Author:
Yiming Yang

Edition 2014

Co-Authors:
Andreas Clementi
Peter Stelzhammer

This case study was funded by AV-Comparatives.

TABLE OF CONTENT

LIST OF FIGURES

LIST OF TABLES

LIST OF ABBREVIATIONS

AV   Anti-Virus

App   Application

COE   Country-of-Origin Effect

PC   Personal Computer

SaaS   Software as a Service

SME   Small and Medium Enterprises

UGC   User Generated Content

VAS   Value-Added Services

MANAGEMENT SUMMARY

This study was initiated for the purpose of investigating the business model which supports Chinese "free" AV-vendors to offer free fully-functional security software.

The study analyzed the business model of two selected Chinese AV-vendors, Qihoo 360 and Baidu, from the perspective of their product development model, revenue model, marketing and distribution, and services and implementation. Furthermore, market research was conducted to compare the Chinese and Western users in order to investigate the influential factors on users' choice of security software.

Key results of the business model analysis

The main challenge of the "free" model is to convert the user base into a commercial value. To achieve this, Qihoo 360 uses its free Internet security products to generate a user base. Second, the company builds a series of channel products, such as a browser and desktop applications, to transform the user base into user traffic, and effectively drive user traffic. Third, the company adopts an advertising revenue model by developing a series of platform products and web services to host online advertising and Internet value-added services (VAS). Finally, through the sales of advertising and Internet VAS, Qihoo 360 generates enough revenue to support its free Internet security products.

User traffic is the key factor for both online advertising and internet VAS. For performance-based advertising, the changes in user traffic directly affect the revenue. For time-based advertising, since the client pays a fixed price to display the ads, the revenue is less susceptible to the change in user traffic. However, the changes in user traffic affect performance of the ads in the long term, and thus, affect the revenue. For internet VAS, user traffic and the quantity of available games on Qihoo 360's game platform are the two main factors which determine the company's overall revenue.

Unlike Qihoo 360, which was originally founded as a software company, Baidu was founded as a search engine provider with a straightforward online advertising business model. The company's revenue performance is mainly based on two factors: user traffic and data managing capacity. The main challenge for Baidu is to maximize the exposure of its advertisements. This was the main incentive for the company to launch its internet security products.

To sum up, the results suggest that the "free" model which the case study companies have applied with their antivirus software is different from the "freemium" model which is commonly practiced by other antivirus vendors outside of China. Qihoo 360 and Baidu generate revenue through their online marketing and internet value-added services (VAS) that are offered for enterprises and other business sectors, while, the "freemium" antivirus vendors generate revenue by cross-selling premium products to users.

For Qihoo 360 and Baidu, the goal is to effectively drive user traffic to support their online advertising service and internet VAS, whereas, for "freemium" antivirus vendors the goal is to convert free users into paying customers.

Key results of market research

The market research was conducted to evaluate whether this "free" model is applicable to non-Chinese markets. The research compared Chinese and Western respondents in regards to users' knowledge of security software, consumer behavior, attitude, future usage intention, and mobile security software usage. Western respondents were mainly European, North-American and Australian.

The primary data of market research was collected through an online questionnaire. The questionnaire was distributed to selected regions. A total of 1,229 responses were received, out of which 972 were valid responses. The "raw" data was analyzed through comparison analysis and cross-tab analysis.

The results of the comparison analysis suggested many differences between Chinese and Western respondents, especially in relation to consumer behavior and their attitude towards security software.

Both Western and Chinese respondents perceive that paid-for security software denotes a better production. However, the Chinese respondents perceived that free security software is more easy to use than paid-for security software, which is exactly opposite to the Western respondents' opinion. Moreover, compared to the Chinese respondents, Western respondents expressed more concerns about the privacy issues regarding the free security software.

Key results:

- 89.9% of Chinese respondents are currently using free security software compared to only 39.3% of Western respondents using free security software.

- Over half of the Chinese respondents (57.0%) and nearly half of the Western respondents (49.1%) would consider the country-of-origin when choosing security software. Western respondents expressed a strong negatively-associated country image towards China.

- The majority of Chinese respondents (58.4%) only used PC security software in the recent five years, compared to 51.4% of Western respondents who had more than 10 years' experience of using security software.

- More than two-thirds of the Chinese respondents (69.2%) are currently using a mobile security app, whereas only 40.9% of Western respondents used a mobile security app.

The cross tab analysis was employed to examine the relationship between users' choice of security software and the factors affecting this such as users' computing habits, demographic background, past experience, and consumer behavior.

The results suggest that the respondents who are retired or work as executives /managers and computer technical/engineers, have a higher percentage of using paid security software. Conversely, respondents who are college/graduate students, or who work as academics/educators and sales/marketing professionals, have a higher percentage of using free security software.

Users' computing habits can also indicate their choice of security software. The respondents who often use electronic banking are more likely to use paid-for security software. The same pattern is also found in online shopping.

The duration that respondents have been using security software is a good predictor of what kind of security software they use. Basically the longer the respondents have been using security software, the more likely they are to use paid-for security software, and vice versa.

Contrary to popular belief, the results imply that the experience of being a victim of cyber-crime does not affect users' choice of security software.

Conclusions

It is still too early to say that "free" is the future of the antivirus industry. The "free" model practiced by Qihoo 360 and Baidu requires various supporting and implementation processes to achieve commercial success. It is hard for a "traditional" software company to build the necessary elements to adopt this model, and it is also difficult for Qihoo 360 and Baidu to achieve commercial value in overseas markets with this model. This is especially true when considering the Western market, where more mature Internet regulations make it more difficult for the case companies to drive user traffic.

The study shows that compared to the Western market, the Chinese market has a higher percentage of smartphone users and a higher usage of mobile security software. This may be due to the lower penetration rate of PC's in China compared to Western countries. Due to the large user traffic potential from mobile devices, it is expected that in the future Chinese free security software vendors will increasingly focus more on the mobile security market.

For international AV-vendors, the study shows that it is difficult to compete with Chinese "free" AV-vendors in the Chinese market of home users. However, because the user traffic is the key to the "free" model, the Chinese free AV-vendors may have less interest in corporate users. Therefore, focusing on corporate users could be an effective strategy for international AV-vendors to establish a presence in the Chinese market. Market research also suggests that there is a market for high-end security software in China, for which people spend more than $56 annually per PC (41.7% of Chinese users who paid for AV spend more than $56 annually per PC).

1. INTRODUCTION

1.1 Background

In the book "Free: The Future of a Radical", Anderson (2009) claims that "every industry that becomes digital, eventually becomes free." Anderson (2009) further explained that because of the development of internet technology, the cost of reaching consumers has dropped dramatically, which is making the whole digital economy cheaper and move closer to free. Zott & Amit (2010) also mentioned in their article that internet users are so used to free web services that they often expect to receive new services and products without any charges. The fundamental question for companies is how to capture commercial value effectively by offering free products and services.

Qihoo 360, a Chinese Internet company founded in 2005, has achieved remarkable success in the retail sector of the Chinese antivirus market by offering free fully-functional antivirus software. Within a decade, Qihoo 360 has become the top internet security software vendor in the Chinese retail market, based on the number of monthly active users (CCID Consulting, 2014a). In early 2013, the company claimed that its user penetration across all of its products was 95.8% of internet users in China (Qihoo 360 Technology Co. Ltd, n.d.).

The company achieved notable popularity not only in the home user sector, but also amongst enterprise and government users. According to the recent research conducted by CCID Consulting[1], Qihoo 360's internet security products have become the most popular products among enterprise users in China with 42% overall user penetration (CCID Consulting, 2014b).

---

[1] A consulting firm affiliated with the China Center for Information Industry Development.

Offering free antivirus software to gain a user base is not a new strategy to the market. International antivirus vendors such as "AVAST"[2] and "AVG"[3] have gained great credit by offering free editions of their antivirus software. However, unlike "AVAST" and "AVG", instead of offering free editions and subsequently gaining from selling paid editions, Qihoo 360 offers free antivirus software with no restricted functions but gains from its advertising and platform services.

After the success of Qihoo 360's free antivirus software, more Chinese antivirus vendors and internet companies begin to offer free fully-functional antivirus products. However, doubts and criticisms have also risen along with the development of free antivirus products. People are not only concerned about free antivirus software's protection performance, but also about the possibility that free vendors misuse their privacy data. Critics accuse the free antivirus vendors of using a "hidden backdoor" or "hidden installation" to take advantage of users' data in order to achieve commercial benefit.

Is the "free" model the future of the antivirus industry or it is simply a particular case of the Chinese market? To answer this question, it is necessary to understand how this "free" model works, and also the particular environment of the Chinese market should be learned. Therefore, this study intends to provide an overview of the Chinese "free" antivirus vendors' business model, and an analysis of the Chinese internet security market.

1.2 Research Objectives

The aim of this research is to investigate the business model of Chinese "free" antivirus software vendors, to identify the relationship between key components of the business model and to analysis the Chinese internet security market.

[2] AVAST Software
[3] AVG Technologies

The objectives include:

i.   To describe the business model of Chinese "free" AV-vendors and establish a comprehensive analysis framework.

ii.   To examine whether this business model can be applied in other markets.

- How hard or easy would it be for Chinese "free" AV vendors to sell their product in international markets, particularly with trust issues and the current business model.

- How hard or easy would it be for International AV vendors to sell their product in Chinese markets, particularly with trust issues and the current business model.

2. METHODOLOGY AND FRAMEWORK

The research was structured in two parts: a case study and a market research.

The case study was carried out using the case study methodology developed by Yin (2009). The studied companies' business model was analyzed according to Rajala et al. (2003)'s software business model analysis framework.

For market research, a questionnaire-based survey was conducted to collect primary data. The questionnaire contained 38 questions with following sections:

- user's knowledge of security software

- consumer behavior and attitudes

- future usage intention

- mobile security software usage

- demography

The primary data was then analyzed through comparison analysis and cross-tab analysis.

2.1 The case study methodology

To provide a detailed description of the studied company's business model is the main focus of this case study research. In addition, the case research is not limited to the studied companies only; the analysis process can be generally applied to software companies for their business model development, and provide guidelines on the innovation process.

2.1.1 Scope

The case study selected two internet security software vendors based on their international or regional market performance and representatives of their business model.

The selected internet security software vendors are:

- **Qihoo 360 Technology Co. Ltd.**, is an internet company based in China. "Qihoo 360 Internet security" is the most popular internet security product in China based on the number of monthly active users (CCID Consulting, 2014a). The company offers its internet and mobile security products free to users.

- **Baidu Inc.** is a Chinese web services company. The company is the leading Chinese-language internet search-engine provider. After progressive acquisitions over the past few years, the company has become the dominant force in many areas, from search engine services to social networking. In 2013, the company announced its first antivirus program "Baidu antivirus". The product was free to users and available in six languages.

2.1.2 Data collection

The data for the case study was gathered mainly via the companies' own communication materials, such as annual and quarterly reports, investor relations, web pages, press releases, product descriptions, and also via trade journals, as well as web-based news services.

2.1.3 Business model analysis framework

The studied company's business model was analyzed based on the business model analysis framework developed by Rajala et al. (2003). This framework was originally developed for the analysis of software businesses, which is suitable for the purpose of this study.

In the paper "A framework for analyzing software business models", Rajala et al. (2003) introduced a framework which contains four elements: product development model, revenue logic, marketing and distribution, and services and implementation (See Figure 2-1).

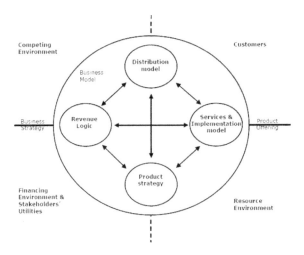

Figure 2-1 Software business model framework (Source: Rajala et al., 2003,)

Product strategy describes the software company's product development model. In other words, it describes the company's core product and service and how the product development work is organized (Rajala et al., 2003). The dimensions of product strategy range from product orientation to service orientation, from customer-specific to standardized (Rajala et al., 2003).

Revenue logic describes the way the software vendors generate their revenue. It includes both sales revenue and other sources of revenue. It is the logic between cost structure and revenue streams (Osterwalder & Pigneur, 2002a). As pointed out by Rajala et al., (2003), the different approaches to capture revenue range from different pricing strategies to different sources of revenue. In the study, Rajala et al., (2003) identified five subcategories of revenue logic for software businesses, which are: cost or value-based pricing, license sales and royalties, revenue sharing, hybrid models and loss-leader pricing[4], and media model.

---

[4] Loss-leader pricing means pricing something for less than its value.

Distribution model describes the marketing and sales strategy of the software companies. This ranges from direct sales to strategic partnerships, and it is tightly interconnected with the product strategy.

Service and implementation model describes the set of services and actions to be implemented. It also describes who carries out these actions. For example, in some cases it was the vendor who installed, configured, and integrated a system for users, whereas in other cases, the customers needed to do complete these tasks by themselves (Rajala et al., 2003).

These four elements were summed up to identify the characteristics of software businesses and help to distinguish the different business models (Rajala et al., 2003).

Rajala et al. (2003) assume factors such as the competition environment, customers, resource environment, financing environment, and corporate and business strategies, function as the given variables which restrict the implementation of various business models. First, a business model is constrained by external variables such as competition environment and customers. Secondly, a business model has to capture and produce the value which is bounded by the financial environment, stakeholder's utilities, and resources (Rajala, Rossi, & Tuunainen, 2003). Third, a business model has to address the strategic objectives set by companies. Finally, the business model is also bounded by the characteristics of the product and service being offered (Rajala et al., 2003).

2.2 The market research methodology

The market research was conducted to find out whether Chinese "free" antivirus vendors' business models could be adopted in the international market. The primary data was collected through a questionnaire-based survey, and the raw data was analyzed through comparison analysis and cross tab analysis.

2.2.1 Questionnaire design

A modified questionnaire was developed with 38 questions, divided into 6 sections (see appendix A-1). The questionnaire obtained information of user's knowledge of security software, consumer behavior, attitude, future usage intention, mobile security software usage, and demography. To maximize the accuracy of the results, multiple question types were applied, such as multiple-choice, rating scale, table of checkboxes, and rankings, etc. Logical links between questions were also adopted (see appendix A-1). The questionnaire was available in both English and Chinese.

A focus group was conducted to test the validity of the questionnaire and to identify the inherent problems before mass distribution of the final questionnaire.

2.2.2 Sampling

The questionnaire was created on the online survey tool SurveyGizmo[5], and distributed by sending an invitation link through various platforms such as email, Facebook, and other social platforms. The questionnaire was conducted between 23rd April 2014 and 13th June 2014. A total of 1,229 responses were received. Out of this number, 972 were valid responses. 34.2% of the responses were from China (including Hong Kong), 33.2 % of responses were from Europe, and 10.5% of the responses were from North America and Australia combined. The online survey tool ensured that no duplicate results were collected.

2.2.3 Data analysis method

The data analysis was separated into two parts:

- The first part was a comparison analysis, where the respondents were segmented into two groups: Chinese respondents and Western respondents,

---

[5] SurveyGizmo is an online survey and data analysis software (http://www.surveygizmo.com/).

according to their demographic data. The objective was to find out how different or similar these two respondent groups were, in terms of user behavior, attitude, and feature usage intention, etc.

- The second part as cross tab analysis; the objective was to find out the factors which influence users' choice of security software.

2.2.4 Statistics

For the comparison analysis, descriptive statistics were employed to describe the samples such as averages and standard deviation. For the cross tab analysis, the testing of statistical significance was employed. The significance level, set at 0.05. P-value, was used to report the data findings.

3. THE CASE STUDY

3.1 Introduction

The study selected two Chinese internet technology companies: Qihoo 360 and Baidu, based on their market performance and representatives of their business model.

The analysis of the case study companies' business models in this chapter is based on Rajala et al.'s (2003) business model framework, which contains four elements: product development model, revenue logic, marketing and distribution, and services and implementation. The analysis is divided according to these four elements. Each element presents a distinct perspective of the case company's business model.

3.2 Qihoo 360 and its business model

3.2.1 Background information of the case study company

Initially, the company focused on selling third-party antivirus software online. In 2006, the company launched its first free security software; 360 Safe Guard. According to the company, 360 Safe Guard gained great popularity in a short time and became the most popular security software in China, in terms of monthly active users (History and Milestones, n.d.).

After establishing a considerable volume of users, the company launched its 360 Application Store in 2008. In the same year, Qihoo 360 introduced its free 360 Safe Browser ("History and Milestones," n.d.).

In October 2009, the company officially launched its 360 Anti-Virus and 360 Mobile Safe app. In the same year, the company achieved 231 million monthly active users across all of its products (CCID Consulting, 2014a).

In 2010, Qihoo 360 became the top vendor of internet security software in China in terms of market penetration (CCID Consulting, 2014a). Likewise, in 2011, the company launched several internet value-added platforms, including a 360 Web Game Browser, 360 Open Platform for Group-Buys, and 360 Application Desktop.

In early 2013, the company claimed that its user penetration across all of its products had reached 95.8% of all internet users in China (Qihoo 360 Technology Co. Ltd, n.d.). In July 2013, the company entered the search engine market with its 360 search service.

According to the company's annual financial reports (Qihoo360 Technology Co. Ltd, n.d.), the sales have doubled every year from 2008-2012, with net benefit showing a similar increase. The company achieved $671.1 million total revenue in 2013, in which the net income was reportedly $99.7 million, showing an increase of 113.2%

from $46.8 million in 2012 (Qihoo 360 Technology Co. Ltd., n.d.).

The products of Qihoo 360 include three layers: a core security layer, an access layer (channel products), and a service layer (platform products).

The core security products are the company's fundamental products, which include:

- **360 Safe Guard** - the company's flagship internet security product offers solutions that include software to help maintain, manage, and secure users' computers. The features also include software update management, resource monitoring and performance optimization, a file download client, and malware scanning (China Stock Research - Qihoo 360 Technologies (QIHU), n.d.).

- **360 Antivirus** – the company's antivirus application scans for and takes corrective action against computer viruses. The product applies multiple antivirus scan engines, which include its own cloud based engines and QVMII engine[6], and third-party scan engines from Avira[7] and Bitdefender[8] (Qihoo 360 Technology Co. Ltd., n.d.).

- **360 Mobile Safe** – this is a security program for the Google Android, Apple iOS, and Nokia Symbian smart phone operating systems. In addition to the traditional antivirus and malware scans, the software can also block spam text messages and incoming calls. The program also has features to optimize phone performance and encrypt data for privacy protection if a phone is lost or stolen (Qihoo 360 Technology Co. Ltd., n.d.)

---

[6] Qihoo Support Vector Machine

[7] Avira is a Germany based multinational antivirus vendor.

[8] Bitdefender antivirus engine is developed by Romania-based software company Softwin.

The products from the access layer content allow users to access the web pages or company's services, which include:

- **360 Browser** – is a web browser developed by Qihoo 360. The features include automatic blocking of malicious websites, and scanning of files downloaded through the browser. The browser also offers a cloud service to store and synchronize bookmarks (China Stock Research - Qihoo 360 Technologies (QIHU), n.d.).

- **360 Desktop** –is a full-screen desktop program that enables users to access their favorite applications, files, and folders, by creating one-click shortcuts. It allows users to search for and obtain both local and web-based applications, and enables direct access to the 360 app store (China Stock Research - Qihoo 360 Technologies (QIHU), n.d.).

- **Mobile Assistant** – is an android-based mobile app store that allows users to download, install, and manage mobile phone applications (China Stock Research - Qihoo 360 Technologies (QIHU), n.d.).

- **Mobile Browser** – is a mobile browser for both android and iOS devices. With a Qihoo ID, users can keep the same web settings and "favorite" folders on both PCs and mobile browsers (Qihoo 360 Technology Co. Ltd., n.d.).

- **Mobile Desktop** – is the mobile versions of the company's desktop programs.

The service layer includes the company's core internet services, which are:

- **360 Personal Start Up Page** – is a start-up page (www.hao.360.cn) filled with links for one-click access to popular web content (news, search engines, e-commerce, games, etc.). The page is the default homepage for the company's browser.

- **360 Search** – is a search engine (www.so.com), developed by Qihoo 360.

Except for general web searches, the company also works with third parties in vertical search channels for results related to certain content types such as videos, music, and maps. The 360 Search is the default search engine for its browser (China Stock Research - Qihoo 360 Technologies (QIHU), n.d.).

- **360 Video** – is a web platform (http://v.360.cn) that enables users to view contents from third-party video sites. The company itself does not host the video, rather it just provides users with categorized links that redirect them to third-party sites (China Stock Research - Qihoo 360 Technologies (QIHU), n.d.).

- **360 Shopping** – is a platform (http://mall.360.cn) that enables users to search and compare the prices of products offered by other e-commerce sites and provides a link to make a purchase (Product&Service, n.d.).

- **360 Game Center** – is a web site (http://g.360.cn) that provides video games for casual and hard-core players. The website contains a selection of popular web games that are operated by third party web game developers. Users can search for video games and follow a link to play on the company's platform or third-party game sites (China Stock Research - Qihoo 360 Technologies (QIHU), n.d.).

In August 2013, the company released its own English language antivirus products: 360 Internet Security 2013, and 360 Mobile Security, targeting international users for the first time. With its global home page (http://www.360safe.com), the company intends to increase its international presence.

In April 2014, the company formed a strategic partnership with Sungy Mobile, a Chinese android mobile service developer. Sungy Mobile's mobile app "GO Launcher" is available in 38 languages in 200 countries, and works as the users' first entry point to their phones (About sungy mobile, n.d.). According to Sungy Mobile, the "GO Launcher" is listed in the top ranking in the Personalization category on

Google Play in over 30 countries (About sungy mobile, n.d.). In 2012, Sungy Mobile opened an office in San Francisco targeting the global market. Qihoo 360 uses Sungy Mobile's app distribution platform to promote its mobile security products.

Despite their commercial success, both criticism and doubt have never ceased to surround Qihoo 360 and its products. In early 2010, Rising, another Chinese antivirus vendor, published an article claiming that 360 Safe Guard has a "Hidden Backdoor" that threatens user's privacy (Lina Wang, 2010). Qihoo 360 reacted by filing a lawsuit against Rising for unfair competition. Although Qihoo 360 eventually won the case, the doubt related to Qihoo 360's"Hidden Backdoor" was widely spread.

In October 2012, an anonymous internet user published a letter titled "Public Letter to MIIT and the Ministry of Public Security for Public whistle-blowing of Qihoo 360" on Sinaweibo (a popular Chinese social network platform). The letter claimed that Qihoo 360's browser contains a "Hidden Backdoor", which threatens both end users' system security and competitor's products and service experience (IDF Laboratory, 2012). An independent research was subsequently conducted by IDF (a technical civil club in China) and indicated that Qihoo 360 browser, indeed, has an undeclared mechanism (i.e., ExtSmartWiz.dll) which connects to the server every 5 minutes. This mechanism can download files from the server, and users are not given any notice when a file is downloaded (IDF Laboratory, 2012). Qihoo 360 later explained that this mechanism downloads the resource files to mitigate a cross site scripting (XSS) vulnerability in a script from Baidu that redirects users to baidu.com if they click upon a Baidu search result from within so.com (IDF Laboratory, 2012). The company further explained that since this mechanism does not upload any data, the users are therefore   unaware of it (IDF Laboratory, 2012).

The following analysis of the case study company's business model is to be based on Rajala et al. (2003)'s business model analysis framework, which comprised product development model, revenue model, marketing and distribution model, and service and implementation model.

3.2.2   Product development model

Qihoo 360's product development process has experienced four stages.

First stage: The company developed its first program, 360 Safe Guard, which works as a PC security assistant tool that can scan for and remove Trojan horse and other malicious code. The program has embedded software management tools that enable other software vendors to promote their software. At this stage Qihoo 360's main business functions are the promotion and distribution of third-party applications. In February 2007, Qihoo formed an alliance with Kaspersky[9] (Chinese subsidiary), which enabled its 360 Safe Guard to be equipped with Kaspersky antivirus software (Sun, 2014). 360 Safe Guard users were given a free half year license to use Kaspersky antivirus software (Sun, 2014). The company also formed similar alliances with NOD32[10] and BitDefender[11].

Second stage: Qihoo 360 launched 360 Antivirus and 360 Mobile Safe. After they successfully gained in user volume from offering the 360 Safe Guard for free, the company decided to launch its own free antivirus software. Promoted with the slogan "permanently free", and with the company's existing user volume, the 360 Antivirus soon became the most popular antivirus software in the Chinese retail market (Iresearch, 2010). Along with the 360 Antivirus, the company launched its free mobile security app, 360 Mobile Safe. At this stage, the company reinforced its presence as an internet security company.

Third stage: Qihoo 360 introduced the 360 Safe Browser, promoted as a more secure browser for users. In 2011, Qihoo 360 provided one year's free remote control

---

[9] A Russian multinational computer security company

[10] Is an antivirus software program developed by Slovakia based IT security company ESET

[11] Is an antivirus software suite developed by Romania-based software company Softwin

computer repair services via 360 Safe Guard, which detailed that when computer repair is necessary, Qihoo 360's engineer would install its browser to the user's PC. The browser served as the main traffic-driving channel to direct users to the company's 360 Personal Start Up Page and 360 search, as those are the default homepage and search engine of the browser.

Fourth stage: The fourth stage was the expansion to platform and web search services. Through the launch of 360 Application Desktop, 360 Web Game Center, 360 Open Platform for Group-Buys, and 360 Search, the company successfully expanded from a distributor of third-party applications to an online advertising and internet VAS provider. This expansion was achieved mostly due to the company's large volume of users gained from its free security products.

From the company's product development path, we can see a logical connection between the company's product development and the growth of its user base. In the early stage, the company developed its foundation products such as 360 Safe Guard and 360 Antivirus to increase their user base. With the growth of user volume, the company developed a series of channel products such as 360 Browser and 360 Desktop, to drive the user traffic. Finally, the company developed a series of platform products and web services to host user traffic (See Figure 3-1). It seems the product development strategy of Qihoo 360 was largely driven by the market, instead of being driven by technology.

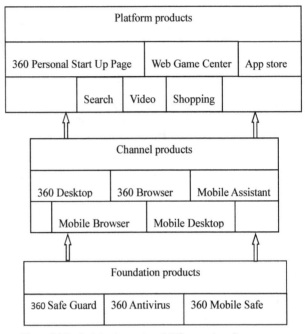

Figure 3-1 Product development model (Own portrayal)

3.2.3 Revenue model

A revenue model consists of revenue streams and cost structure. The revenue streams are a set of different pricing mechanisms (Klein & Loebbecke, 2000). The cost structure measures all the costs which the firm has to account for to create a market and deliver value. A good revenue model translates the firms' value proposition into a set of revenue streams, and balances this with its cost structure (Osterwalder & Pigneur, 2002b).

3.2.3.1 Revenue streams

The case study company's revenue model consists of multiple revenue streams. The company's two main revenue streams are online advertising and internet value-added services (VAS). In 2012, online advertising contributed 67% of the company's total revenue, and the internet value-added services accounted for 31% of the company's total revenue (China Stock Research - Qihoo 360 Technologies (QIHU), n.d.).

The online advertising revenue is driven by the company's online marketing and search referral services. Online marketing services include paid links placed on the company's web sites which link to clients' sites or applications hosted on Qihoo 360's platform products ("China Stock Research - Qihoo 360 Technologies (QIHU)," n.d.). The price of an advertisement is based on time and performance. The performance-based pricing is based on the measurable metrics such as cost-per-click. The time-based pricing is charged by the amount of time for which the advertisement has been displayed. The price is determined partly by the client's industry and the location of the advertisement on the page. In the annual report of 2013, the company claimed, in addition to the 360 Personal Startup Page, the company's search and mobile services web sites also provided incremental growth for the advertising revenues (Qihoo 360 Technology Co. Ltd. Fourth Quarter and FY 2013, n.d.).

Search referral services are the search traffic that are sent to third-party search engines for processing. The majority of search referral revenues are contributed by Google. However, after the company launched its 360 Search in 2012, Qihoo 360 and Google have terminated their relationship ("China Stock Research - Qihoo 360 Technologies (QIHU)," n.d.).

User traffic and ad clicks are key variables for understanding the Online Advertising industry (Evans, 2009). The case study company reveals both the number of daily unique visitors to its 360 Start-Up Page, and the number of ad clicks on the page (see Figure 3-2). Unique visitors can be defined as a solitary session of a user on a web page. Theoretically, the same person can account for multiple unique visits in a single day. Ad clicks measures the total number of times that a user clicks an advertisement link, which is a more straightforward measurement ("China Stock Research - Qihoo 360 Technologies (QIHU)," n.d.).

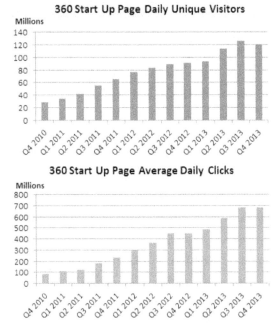

Figure 3-2 Daily unique visitors and daily clicks
(Source: China Stock Research - Qihoo 360 Technologies)

The increase of unique visitors is mostly contributed by the company's release of its PC browser and mobile browser, which drives a huge amount of user traffic to the 360 Start Up Page as it is the default home page of its browser. As shown by Figure 3-2, the average daily clicks have increased in a similar fashion as the increase of unique visitors, and the number of clicks per user actually shows that users are clicking more ("China Stock Research - Qihoo 360 Technologies (QIHU)," n.d.).

Internet value-added services (VAS) are the case study company's other main revenue source. The internet VAS are mainly provided through the company's various platforms. The services includes providing third-party games on the company's game center platform, providing third-party apps through the company's app store, and providing remote technical support and other services.

According to the company's annual report, game platforms contribute to a large part of its internet VAS revenue. The company's game platform hosts third-party developed games and provides users with a secure gaming environment. The company hosted over 110 games on its platform in the year 2012. The company shares revenues with third-party game developers and earns a portion of what players spend on in-game purchases ("China Stock Research - Qihoo 360 Technologies (QIHU)," n.d.).

The games attract both causal and hard-core players. Most games on the company's platform have a lifespan of 3-28 months. In 2012, the top ten games contributed about 55% of the total game revenue.

From May 2012, the company started offering its remote technical support free to users. The company also established its "geek" platform, whereby qualified independent IT technicians can offer their services through the Qihoo 360 geek platform.

Other services include payment and billing services in which the company acts as a third-party payment and settlement provider, and takes a commission based on the gross amount collected or disbursed ("China Stock Research - Qihoo 360 Technologies (QIHU)," n.d.).

Based on the company's annual report from 2013, the total revenues in 2013 were $671.1 million. Online advertising revenues were $417.1 million, and the internet VAS revenues were $252.7 million (Qihoo 360 Technology Co. Ltd. Fourth Quarter and FY 2013, n.d.).

User traffic is the key factor for both online advertising and internet VAS. In other words, the user traffic greatly determines the case study company's revenue.

The advertising revenues include performance-based advertising as well as time-based advertising, and user traffic affects these differently ("China Stock Research - Qihoo 360 Technologies (QIHU)," n.d.). For performance-based advertising, the changes in user traffic directly affect the revenue. For time-based advertising, since the client pays a fixed price to display the ads, the revenue is less susceptible to the change in user traffic. However, the changes in user traffic affect performance of the ads in the long term, and thus, affect the revenue.

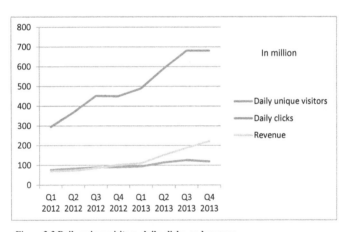

Figure 3-3 Daily unique visitors, daily clicks, and revenue
(Own portrayal, data derived from Qihoo 360 Quarter Reports, Qihoo 360 Technologies)

As shown in the figure above, the slight decrease of daily unique visitors between third quarter and fourth quarter of 2013 did not affect the increase in revenue. However, it may affect the revenues in the long run if daily unique visitors continue to drop.

For internet VAS, the revenue is dependent on the following variables: number of players, percentage of what players will pay, average amount spent on games, and

company's share of revenue from third-party developers ("China Stock Research -
Qihoo 360 Technologies (QIHU)," n.d.). Assuming the amount of spending is
relatively constant for each player, the number of players becomes the main factor.
Based on the company's data, the number of players depends on the number of
games available ("China Stock Research - Qihoo 360 Technologies (QIHU)," n.d.).
Therefore, the number of games on the company's platform is the main variable
which affects the company's internet VAS revenue.

To sum up, user traffic and the quantity of available games on Qihoo 360's game
platform are the two main factors which determine the company's overall revenue.

3.2.3.2 Cost structure

Due to the character of the business's service, the costs of revenue for the case study
company are relatively low. According to the company's annual report (2013), the
cost of revenues in 2013 was $87.8 million, and the revenue was $671.1 million
(Qihoo 360 Technology Co. Ltd. Fourth Quarter and FY 2013, n.d.). The direct costs
include bandwidth costs, web hosting equipment and engineers, business tax, VAT,
traffic acquisition costs, and payment collection costs ("China Stock Research -
Qihoo 360 Technologies (QIHU)," n.d.).

The company has relatively large operational costs (see Table 3-1). According to the
company's statements of operations, the operating costs in 2013 were $482.5 million,
which include selling and marketing, general and administrative, and product
development (Qihoo 360 Technology Co. Ltd. Fourth Quarter and FY 2013, n.d.).

Among the above mentioned costs, product development expenditure was accounted
for more than half of the total operating costs, with $225.2 million expenses in 2013
(Qihoo 360 Technology Co. Ltd. Fourth Quarter and FY 2013, n.d.).

The expansion of product development is mainly towards the company's free
software offerings such as 360 Safe Guard, 360 Antivirus, browser, and mobile apps.

As explained by the product development model, these software help to build the user base and drive user traffic, since the user traffic is the main factor which affects the company's revenue. Therefore, the product development expenses are indirectly important to increase the company's revenue (See Figure 3-4).

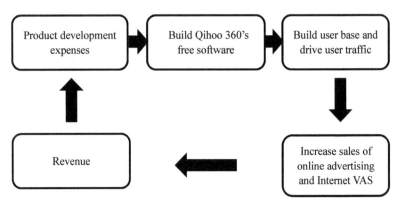

Figure 3-4 Product development expenses cycle (Own portrayal)

Operating costs In thousands USD	2009	2010	2011	2012	2013
Selling and marketing	6,256	12,603	46,836	58,178	110,104
General and administrative	2,531	5,051	19,054	34,295	116,200
Product development	10,664	24,505	64,962	156,269	255,248
Percentage of sales					
Selling and marketing	19%	22%	28%	18%	16%
General and administrative	8%	9%	11%	10%	17%
Product development	33%	42%	39%	47%	38%

Table 3-1 Operating costs analysis (Source: China Stock Research)

3.2.3.3 The logic between revenue streams and cost structure

To understand the logic between the case study company's revenue streams and cost structure, it is necessary to combine the results with the company's product model. As shown in Table 3-1, the company spent a large amount of its revenue on product development in order to offer free software products and update the software. In return, the free software encourages an increase of the company's user base, and acts like a promotion channel to increase market awareness. In the next stage, the company spends money on the promotion of its browser, desktop, and mobile apps in order to drive the user traffic toward its platform products. In the final stage, the company spends money on building and maintaining its platform products to host its online advertising and internet VAS.

User traffic is therefore the key factor affecting the company's revenue sources. The company's main costs are necessary for the development and maintenance of its foundation products and channel products, which are the main instruments to increase user traffic. Therefore, we can conclude that user traffic is the connection between the company's revenue streams and cost structure (see Figure 3-5).

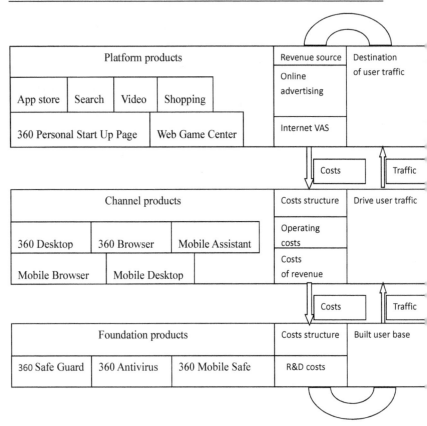

Figure 3-5 The revenue model (Own portrayal)

3.2.4   Marketing and distribution model

Established in 2005, the case study company initially used word of mouth to promote its 360 Safe Guard and expand its user base. The free product and service of the case study company received positive feedback from the users.

There are mainly two groups of customers: First, for the company's software products the target market includes PC users, internet users, game players, and smart phone users. Second, for the company's online advertising and internet VAS, the target market is primarily commercial companies and third-party partners including app developers, game developers, and search engine providers.

In terms of software products, after the initial stage based on word of mouth promotion, the company launched its TV commercials on China's central television (CCTV) network with the slogan "permanently free" to increase its brand awareness. 'Permanently free' is also the company's main promotion strategy. Furthermore, the company promotes its software through software downloading platform providers and online advertisers.

Third-party partnership is another key promotion channel for the case study company's products, for example the partnerships with both Kaspersky Lab and Google during the early stages. Recently, however, the company has formed a partnership with Sungy Mobile in which the company will leverage Sungy Mobile's distribution network to reach mobile users through Sungy Mobile's platform products. Moreover, distribution through the company's own platforms also contributes to a large part of the product distribution, for example, the company will recommend its new products to existing users.

In terms of online advertising service, Qihoo 360's marketing platform (http://e.360.cn/) and its toll-free sales hotline are the main communication channels to reach potential clients. Qihoo 360 also promotes and distributes its online advertising service through agents in 25 provinces of China. The agents are mostly local marketing and promotion companies. The company also hosts marketing conferences to promote its online advertising service. For example, in 2014, the company hosted the "One So, One Win" conference targeting small and medium enterprises (SMEs) in 20 major cities throughout China (Qihoo 360 Technology Co., Ltd., marketing platform, n.d.). Consequently, the number clients of the company's online advertising service has increased along with the growth of the company's web site and web search services (See Table 3-2).

Customer Data Online Advertising	2009	2010	2011	2012	2013
Total Customer Count	139	210	350	860	50,000
Revenue Contribution of Top Five	27.8%	35.1%	27.9%	21.3%	15.6%

Table 3-2 Customer data (Source: China Stock Research)

In terms of internet VAS, Qihoo 360 mainly uses its open platform home page (http://open.360.cn/) to service the game and app developers. The platform home page lists all current platforms which the company operates.

For game developers, Qihoo 360's open game platform (open.1360.com) is the main communication channel. Developers can apply and submit their games through this open game platform. Qihoo 360 will evaluate the games and publish the qualifying games on its game center. Recently, to encourage mobile game developers, the case study company applied a series of promotions, including a free 10-day-promotion service and assistant service for new games. In addition, for the new mobile games, the case study company does not take a share of the revenue during first three months, if the game's monthly revenue is less than 500,000 RMB (80,291 USD) (Qihoo 360 Technology Co. Ltd. Open platform, n.d.). Moreover, the company also launched its English language developer platform (http://developer.360.cn/), with an "all-in-one" service for PC, mobile, and web game developers.

For app developers, the main channel is through the company's open app platform. Developers can use this platform for web or mobile apps. The process is similar to the game platform; developers can apply and submit their app through this open app platform, and the case study company will evaluate and publish the app.

In conclusion, the marketing and distribution model of the case study company is relatively complicated. The company heavily relies on its own platforms to promote and distribute its products and services. The company has two target markets, comprising its users and customers. The "user segment" includes the users of the company's free software or platform products, such as security software, PC management software, and its game center. Here, it is important to note that, most users do not pay for the company's products since they are mostly free. The "customer segment" includes the clients of the company's online advertising service, and internet VAS services, which are paid-for services.

To increase the volume of users, the company took advantage of offering free products, and used word of mouth, TV commercials, and third party patterns to promote and distribute their free software (See Figure 3-6). The result was quite remarkable. Within a short time, the company gained great popularity due to its free software products.

To increase the number of customers, the company relied heavily on its own platform to promote itself to developers (See Figure 3-6). For the online advertising service, the company used multiple channels such as platform, agent, and promotional conferences to reach their enterprising customers (See Figure 3-6).

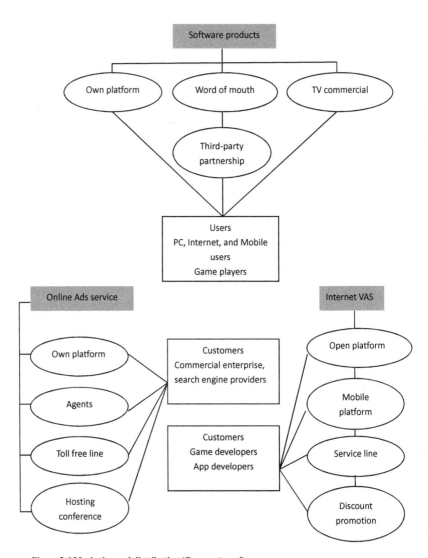

Figure 3-6 Marketing and distribution (Own portrayal)

3.2.5   Service and implementation model

Depending on the product of the company, the implementation process is very different. For the software products, the implementation is relatively simple. Users can choose and download products through the company's product page (http://www.360.cn/) or its global page (http://www.360safe.com/), or through third party downloading websites and app stores. By installing the products, users agree to comply with the user agreement. Users can also create a user account, and benefit from more internet services. However, this feature is optional for users.

On the other hand, the implementation processes of the company's online advertising service and internet VAS are fairly complicated. This is because these two services involve the process of application, evaluation, data analysis, customization, and payment method, etc.

For internet VAS, the process starts with the application, for which the developers need to create an account on 360 open platforms. For enterprises, the clients need to submit their enterprise information, including their Business License number. The case study company will then examine the customers' information and allow access if the customer is qualified. A similar process applies to private developers, for which the developers have to submit their information, including identity information. The company will then issue access to the qualified developers. With the access issued by the case study company, clients can create and manage their apps or games on the case study company's platform.

After the developer creates its apps or games, the company will examine the product through its database. The qualifying products will be published within one hour. As for the unqualified products, the company will give notice to the client, explain the reasoning, and also provide suggestions for improvement. The customers can also use the company's "cloud test" service to test the product's performance in a real user environment. Payment is made through the case study company's payment system. Basically, the game players charge credit on the case study company's platform and consume credit within the games. The company will then transport the credit to the game developer's account according to the revenue-share agreement.

For the online advertising service, the company has two types of pricing. These include performance-based pricing and time-based pricing. The price is also determined by the clients' industry. The process starts with a request from a client. Clients can make a request through the company's marketing platform, agents, or customer service hotline. If the request is made through the company's marketing platform, the process will be similar to that of internet VAS. First the client creates an account on the marketing platform and inputs their basic information, and then the company's sales team contacts the client to discuss the request and quotes the relevant price (Qihoo 360 Technology Co. Ltd. Marketing platform, n.d.). The client can make a request and order advertising services directly with the local agents. The client can also call the company's customer service hotline to make a request for services.

The payment is processed through the company's marketing platform. This will be charged automatically according to the price agreed. Customers can also set a daily limit, if it is performance-based pricing (priced per click), in which, if the click payment reaches their daily payment limit, the ads will go off-line on that day. Through their account, customers can review the payment information and request an invoice.

To conclude, the implementation process is fairly simple for the company's software products (See Figure 3-7).

For the internet VAS, the main implementation effort is on examining and evaluating the third party developers. The company has developed an examination and payment system (See Figure 3-7) to ensure an effective process.

For the online advertising service, the main implementation effort is on
customization, in which the company must cultivate a well-trained sales team. In
addition, the company developed its marketing platform to increase the effectiveness
of management and encourage smooth payment (See Figure 3-7).

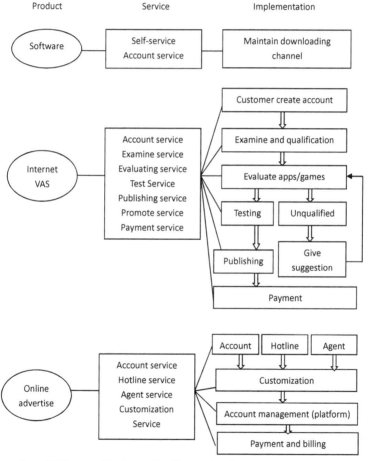

Figure 3-7 Service and implementation (Own portrayal)

3.2.6   Summary of the case analysis

In summary, the analysis of the case study company's business model in this section is based on Rajala et al. (2003)'s business model analysis framework, which contains four elements: product development, revenue logic, marketing and distribution, and services and implementation. The analysis is divided according to these four elements and each element presents a distinct perspective of the case company's business model.

The product development model of the case company is relatively complicated as the company offers three distinct "product groups". The first group comprises the company's foundation software products which are 360 Safe Guard, 360 Antivirus, and mobile security apps. These products are offered for free to the users. The second group consists of the company's channel software products such as 360 Browser and 360 Desktop, etc. The reason for calling these channel products is because these products are recommended by the company's foundation products and act as a channel to drive the user traffic towards the company's platform products. The last product group includes the company's platform products, such as the 360 game center and 360 app store, etc. Through these platform products, the company can present its online advertising service and internet VAS, which are the main revenue generating sources for the company.

The revenue model is the logic between revenue stream and cost structure (Osterwalder & Pigneur, 2002b). For the case study company, the revenue streams mainly consist of the online advertising service and internet VAS. The cost structure mainly consists of revenue costs and operation costs. The main factor determining the case study company's revenue performance is the level of user traffic. A change in user traffic will either directly or indirectly affect the company's revenue. To increase revenue, the company needs to constantly increase user traffic. Since user traffic is determined by the performance of the company's foundation and channel software products, the company therefore needs to constantly invest in the development of software products. In this way, the logic between Qihoo 360's revenue stream and their cost structure is clear. The revenue which comes from online advertising services and internet VAS is spent mostly on the company's free software products to maintain and increase the user traffic (See Figure 3-5).

Marketing and distribution model is constructed according to the company's target markets. There are two different target markets; the Internet users, and the enterprises, including game or app developers. The company has developed various channels and strategies to address these two target markets (See Figure 3-6). For the user market, Qihoo 360 used the advantage of being free, and utilized word of mouth, TV commercials, and third party patterns to promote and distribute its free software. For the enterprise market, Qihoo 360 relies heavily on its own platforms and multiple channels, such as agent sand promotional conferences, to reach potential enterprises and developers (See Figure 3-6)

Service and implementation model is the last element according to the software business model analysis framework (Rajala et al., 2003). Due to the case study company's different product groups, the services and implementation processes are very different. For the software products, the implementation process is relatively simple, where users themselves are the main parties taking action, since they need to download and install the software by themselves (See Figure 3-7). For the company's online advertising services and internet VAS, the implementation process is relatively complicated. It involves application, evaluation, data analysis, customization, and payment method, etc. (See Figure 3-7). The main implementation effort is employed to examine and evaluate the third party developers and customization for online advertising services.

In conclusion, Qihoo 360's business model is not new to the market; many of the elements such as revenue model and implementation model are widely applied in internet companies. However, the way in which Qihoo 360 organized each element and the fitness of the architecture it created is quite remarkable. The successful combination of Internet business with software business, and the creation of a good fit for the two, required a notable amount of innovation at multiple levels. Therefore, the case study company's business model can be seen as an innovation for the software industry, especially for the internet security industry. Moreover, the case study company's business model is different and required various supporting implementation processes which make it hard to be replicated by other software companies.

However, it is important to note that since Qihoo 360's revenue and implementation model are similar to internet businesses, this model is therefore fairly easy for internet companies to adopt. This may partially explain why the new Chinese free antivirus software vendors are mostly from internet information services companies, such as Baidu[12] and Tencent[13].

---

[12] Baidu, a Chinese web services company

[13] China's largest Internet Company, services include social networks, web portals, e-commerce, and online games, etc.

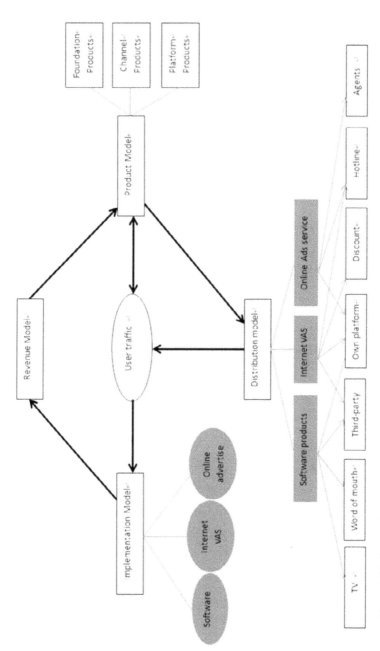

Figure 3-8 Business model of Qihoo 360 (Own portrayal)

3.3 Baidu and its business model

3.3.1 Background information of the case company

Baidu Inc. (Baidu) is a Chinese Internet company founded in 2000. The company, which is known for its Chinese language-search engine service, has grown to become the leading Chinese language-search engine provider, accounting for 79% of the search-engine market share in China ("China Search Engine Marketing Q1 2014," n.d.). In addition to the search engine service, the company offers various user products such as Social Networking Products, user generated content (UGC) products, Online Maps, and software products, including security products ("China Stock Research - Baidu Inc. (BIDU)," n.d.).

Like other companies in the same sector, Baidu provides its user products free to users, and the company generates its revenue through online advertising service. Initially, the company was focused on its search engine and related services,; however, the company has recently expanded its product range into entertainment, social, mobile platforms, and internet security. The company also expanded to hardware products, such as low-cost smart phones ("Baidu releases cheap smartphone," n.d.).

In 2013, Baidu launched its first antivirus software "Baidu Antivirus" targeting the Southeast Asian market. The core technology of "Baidu Antivirus" is based on an "anti-spyware toolkit" developed by Qianyun network technology co. Ltd, and was bought by Baidu in 2012 ("Baidu announce free antivirus software," 2013). In the same year, Baidu announced its second antivirus software "Baidu Shadu" targeting only the domestic market. "Baidu Shadu" is jointly developed by Baidu and Kaspersky Lab ("Baidu launches official antivirus software with Kaspersky," n.d.). Both antivirus products are permanently free to users.

In the first quarter of 2014, the company reported $1.528 billion of revenue ("First

Quarter 2014 Results", Baidu, Inc., n.d.). The company's annual revenue in 2013 was $5.2 billion with a net income of $1.71 billion ("Baidu Inc. ADS," n.d.).

According to the recent ranking of the world's largest internet companies, in terms of market value, Baidu stands as the 7th largest internet company in the world ("Top internet companies, n.d.).

3.3.2   Product development model

The case study company's products and services can be categorized into two segments, the user products and services, and online marketing services, similar to Google. Each of the segments contains a vast amount of different products. This section of the paper will present Baidu's current products according to the products segments.

3.3.2.1 The user products and services

The majority of the user products are related to the company's core product i.e., the web search engine, which includes web search, image search, video search, news, dictionary, user generated content, home page, etc. ("Products," 2014). The company's core product strategy is to offer as many user products as possible, to maintain a large user base ("China Stock Research - Baidu Inc. (BIDU)," n.d.).

The company's user products can be divided into six groups according to the character of the products, which are, search products, social networking products, user generated content (UGC) products, location-based products, software products, and platform products ("China Stock Research - Baidu Inc. (BIDU)," n.d.).

After establishing the products and services around the company's core search service, Baidu entered the software industry, by launching various software products including:

- **Baidu Antivirus**: A permanently free antivirus software for international users. The product's core was developed by Qianyun network technology co. Ltd, and bought by Baidu in 2013. Baidu Antivirus applied a local proactive defense plus cloud proactive defense to the Avira antivirus engine. The product is available in English, Thai, Portuguese, Indonesian, Spanish, Simplified Chinese, and Traditional Chinese. Currently, the product is only available for Windows Operating Systems.

- **Baidu Shadu**: A permanently free antivirus software developed by Baidu. The product is equipped with Baidu's own cloud and local antivirus scan engine and Kaspersky antivirus engine.

- **Mobile Guardian**: A free security software for mobile devices. Besides the antivirus function, the product also provides system optimization, data protection, and call blocking functions ("China Stock Research - Baidu Inc. (BIDU)," n.d.).

- **Guard**: is a PC management software that provides system optimization, software management, and security maintenance functions ("China Stock Research - Baidu Inc. (BIDU)," n.d.).

- **Media Player:** a music and video player for streaming and offline viewing ("China Stock Research - Baidu Inc. (BIDU)," n.d.).

The company's platform products include:

- **Hao123.com**: a personal start-up page that includes search capabilities and a collection of popular web links. This is the largest start-up page in China in terms of user traffic.

- **Baidu App store:** provides a vast collection of third party applications.

- **Baidu Games**: a web game platform providing users with a collection of web games. Users can search for and play games on the platform.

- **91 Wireless**: a mobile app marketplace and mobile game operator.

- **QuNar**: a travel-related information and e-commerce website. The website is not a travel agency, but a platform for third party travel agencies. Users can search for airline tickets, hotel rooms, vacation packages, and attraction tickets through the website. QuNar is a Baidu subsidiary ("China Stock Research - Baidu Inc. (BIDU)," n.d.).

- **Nuomi**: a website offering group buy discounts. It allows users to aggregate their purchasing power to receive discounts on different purchases, which mostly include entertainment, dining, and health and beauty products ("China Stock Research - Baidu Inc. (BIDU)," n.d.).

To summarize, from this range of products, we can see the majority of the company's user products are search products and platform products. This can also indicate the company's focus on their user product development.

3.3.2.2 The online marketing services

As compared to the vast range of Baidu's user products, the company's online marketing services display a different picture with more focus and less variety.

The case study company's online marketing services include:

- **Search Query**: a keyword-based online marketing service which is a common method for the search engine companies. The clients' advertisements will show up to the users who use Baidu's search engine, according to the search key word. Baidu offers two types of keyword-based advertising: performance based and BrandZone. The performance-based pricing measures the advertisement exposure based on clicks (cost-per-click). The BrandZone service includes the provision of specific content based on a brand name keyword ("China Stock Research - Baidu Inc. (BIDU)," n.d.).

For example, if users search Dell, the Dell's store location, new PC model, and other supporting results will show up in BrandZone section.

- **Contextual**: a content-based advertising service, in which Baidu displays the advertising on Baidu's various platforms according to the contents of the advertisements. This service requires a more complicated technology than for the search query. The effectiveness of this service depends on the case study company's capacity to analyze data. ("China Stock Research - Baidu Inc. (BIDU)," n.d.).

- **Audience Attributes**: a marketing service, in which the client's advertisements can be displayed according to the targeted demographic segment. Baidu also calls this service Targetizement or Grand Media solutions.

- **Display placements:** a time-based advertising service, through which the case study company can display client's advertisement on the agreed platform website with an agreed time and location on the page.

- **Value added service (VAS):** In addition to the advertising services, the company also offers different internet VAS through its various platforms such as game platform, app store, group buy, and travel information platform.

Overall, the company's online marketing services are developed along with its search engine services and data management capacity.

3.3.3 Revenue model

3.3.3.1 Revenue streams

According to the case company's annual report, the company's revenue streams consist of two services group: online marketing services and other services (Baidu, Inc., n.d.). Most of the revenue is generated through online marketing services which contributed 99.6% of the company's total revenue in 2013 (See Table 3-3).

Baidu Inc. Revenue Mix (000) RMB	2009	2010	2011	2012	2013
Online marketing services	4,445,310	7,912,869	14,489,767	22,245,643	31,802,219
Other services	2,466	2,205	11,019	60,383	141,705
Total revenue	4,447,776	7,915,074	14,500,786	22,306,026	31,943,924
Mix					
Online marketing services	99.9%	100.0%	99.9%	99.7%	99.6%
Other services	0.1%	0.0%	0.1%	0.3%	0.4%

Table 3-3 Baidu Revenue mix (Source: China Stock Research - Baidu Inc.)

The key services of online marketing include the company's various online advertising services, such as search queries, contextual, audience attributes, display placements, and other forms. The company's pricing strategy includes cost per click pricing, display pricing, and cost per action pricing (clients pay for users' action, for example each phone call, inquiry) ("China Stock Research - Baidu Inc. (BIDU)," n.d.). Similar to Qihoo 360, user traffic is the key factor that determines the price and performance of the advertisements. In other words, this factor determines the company's revenue.

Another source of revenue for the case company is its "Other services", which include certification services, Baidu Credit, group buy, and consulting services. However, these services are insignificant in terms of their percentage in total revenue.

3.3.3.2 Cost structure

The cost structure of the case company consists of revenue costs and fixed costs. The revenue costs consist of traffic acquisition costs, bandwidth costs, equipment costs, compensation costs, tax, etc. The fixed costs are mainly marketing costs, administrative costs, and research and development costs ("China Stock Research - Baidu Inc. (BIDU)," n.d.).

For revenue costs, the largest of these was the cost of traffic acquisition, which consumed 12% of the company's total revenue in 2013 (See Table 3-4). The traffic acquisition costs are mainly the portion of revenue paid to the case study company's partners in exchange for directing traffic.

Baidu Inc. Cost of Revenues (000) RMB	2009	2010	2011	2012	2013
Sales tax and surcharges	-275,924	-504,846	-1,024,858	-1,572,420	-2,329,558
Traffic acquisition costs	-697,673	-758,078	-1,155,546	-1,929,966	-3,704,146
Bandwidth costs	-203,927	-310,540	-626,444	-1,069,306	-1,938,520
Depreciation of servers and other equipment	-250,969	-331,685	-657,845	-1,062,060	-1,469,646
Operational costs	-181,369	-208,035	-358,169	-589,555	-1,175,624
Content costs		-29,802	-66,494	-215,133	-830,369
Shared-based compensation costs	-6,374	-6,302	-7,527	-10,105	-23,976
Costs as a percent of total revenue					
Sales tax and surcharges	6%	6%	7%	7%	7%
Traffic acquisition costs	16%	10%	8%	9%	12%
Bandwidth costs	5%	4%	4%	5%	6%
Depreciation of servers and other equipment	6%	4%	5%	5%	5%
Operational costs	4%	3%	2%	3%	4%
Other	0%	0%	1%	1%	3%

Table 3-4 Baidu Cost of revenues (Source: China Stock Research - Baidu Inc.)

For fixed costs, the largest amount of expenses comes from marketing and R&D, which together spent 26% of the company's total revenue in 2013 (See Table 3-5). R&D spending is the key factor for Baidu, since both the user traffic and advertisement exposure are affected by the company's user products and data analysis technology ("China Stock Research - Baidu Inc. (BIDU)," n.d.).

Baidu Inc. Fixed costs (000) RMB	2009	2010	2011	2012	2013
Selling and marketing	-573,088	-778,353	-1,216,718	-1,841,590	-4,012,709
General and administrative	-230,900	-310,627	-476,092	-659,746	-1,160,824
Research and development	-422,615	-718,038	-1,334,434	-2,304,825	-4,106,832
Fixed costs as a percent of revenue					
Selling and marketing	13%	10%	8%	8%	13%
General and administrative	5%	4%	3%	3%	4%
Research and development	10%	9%	9%	10%	13%

Table 3-5 Baidu Fixed cost (Source: China Stock Research - Baidu Inc.)

In conclusion, Baidu applied a standard internet company revenue model which is based on user traffic and quality of advertisement exposure (See Figure 3-9).

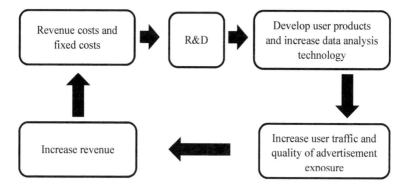

Figure 3-9 Revenue model of Baidu (Own portrayal)

3.3.4 Marketing and distribution model

There are two main target markets of the case study company: web users, and enterprises. The two target markets have different characteristics; therefore, they will be addressed separately.

For web services, Baidu mainly uses its own search page to promote its search related products, social networking products, and platform products. Baidu also launched a TV commercial that was aired on China central television (CCTV) to increase the overall brand awareness, rather than promoting a particular product. For software products, Baidu relies heavily on its own platform and search engine for promotion and distribution. The company also uses its partners' platforms such as application download platforms and IT home pages (See Figure 3-10).

For online marketing services, the main channel is through the company's "Baidu promote" (http://e.baidu.com/) platform, and toll-free sales hotline. The link of "Baidu promote" is directly under the company's search page. Another promoting channel is the company's "Baidu union" service. Baidu union is a service which the case study company provides to its corporate users. Enterprises can join Baidu union and benefit from the data and information services. Moreover, the case study company promotes itself through its agents across major provinces in China, as well as in other countries and regions such as Korea, Japan, Taiwan, Thailand, Malaysia, and Holland. In addition, the company also provides consulting and training services (See Figure 3-10).

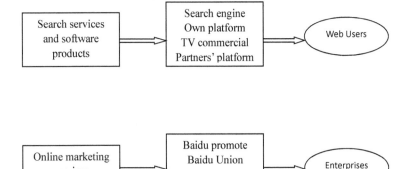

Figure 3-10 Marketing and distribution model of Baidu (Own portrayal)

3.3.5   Service and implementation model

The service and implementation model is determined by the company's different products and customers. For the company's search and software products, the implementation is fairly simple as most of the processes encourage users to avail a system of self-service. However, the company's online marketing service requires much higher implementation and management capacity (See Figure 3-11).

The process starts with the clients' request for the advertising service. The clients can place a request through the case study company's sales hotline, marketing platform, or local agents. Clients can also leave the request on the case study company's marketing platform under "note" function, after which, the sales team will contact the clients. The pricing for online advertising is based on performance (cost-per-click); the cost for each click is dependent on the keyword and the industry of the customer. Moreover, the company has applied a bid price system, through which the customer can place a bid for keywords. The level of bid will be the one factor that would affect ads exposure ("Baidu Promote, pricing," n.d.). In the next stage, the case study company's sales team will assist the customer with the designing of the advertising plan and agree upon a certain price.

Following this, customers are required to load a certain amount of credit, depending on the advertising plan, and the company will issue them with an account for "Baidu promote". The contract and agreement will be signed at this stage. With the account, the customer can manage their advertisement, keywords, and set a daily or weekly budget. The BrandZone and Baidu union services also come under the company's marketing platform. Customers can choose these services through the same process (See Figure 3-11).

Product   Service   Implementation

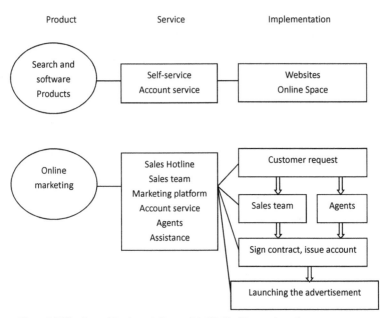

Figure 3-11 Service and implementation model of Baidu (Own portrayal)

3.3.6 Summary of the case analysis

Baidu was founded as a search engine provider, with a classical internet company business model. The company's revenue performance is mainly based on two factors: user traffic and data managing capacity. User traffic determines the price of the advertisements which the company can sell. The data managing capacity determines the quality of advertising performance, since it requires an advanced computing power to deliver better matching of the keywords and to understand users' behavior. Therefore, the R&D expense is a main influencing factor in the company's cost structure, and is also the main factor to gain the competitive advantage.

To maintain their position as market leader and deal with the emerging competitors in the company's core search business, the company applied a product expansion strategy through which the company offers as many users services as possible that most internet users frequently use ("China Stock Research - Baidu Inc. (BIDU)," n.d.).

3.4 Summary of the case study

The case study analyzed the business model of two selected case companies: Qihoo 360 and Baidu. The study has analyzed four elements of the business model according to Rajala et al. (2003)'s software business model analysis framework. The elements of the framework are product development model, revenue model, marketing and distribution model, and service and implementation model. Each of the elements has been analyzed in detail, and combined are able to present the whole pictures of the case study companies' business models.

Qihoo 360 was founded as a software company which focuses on security products. After the initial success as a third-party platform provider, the company realized its potential to gain a broad user base by offering free security software. The main challenge was to devise a business model to turn the user base into commercial value. To achieve this, first Qihoo 360 established a product development model which has a specifically designed product range to turn the user base into user traffic and effectively drive user traffic (See Figure 3-1). Second, to capture the commercial value, the company adopted the advertising revenue model which is commonly used in the internet industry (See Figure 3-5). Third, the company established an effective marketing and implementation model to maximize value. The key challenge of Qihoo 360's business model is to effectively integrate the software business model and internet advertising business model. To achieve this, the company is required to strike a balance between each of the four elements (See Figure 3-8).

Unlike Qihoo 360, which was originally founded as a software company, Baidu was founded as a search engine provider with a straightforward online advertising business model. The main challenge for Baidu is to expand its user base and maximize the exposure of its advertisements ("China Stock Research - Baidu Inc. (BIDU)," n.d.). To achieve this, the company developed an "expansion" product development model. In other words, Baidu offers a lot of products that internet users frequently use, and constantly expands its product range ("China Stock Research - Baidu Inc. (BIDU)," n.d.). This was the main incentive for the company to launch its internet security products. The company's revenue model is largely based on the company's online advertising business. The marketing and implementation model is also established to support this core business.

To sum up, the results suggest that the "free" model which the case study companies have applied with their antivirus software is different from the "freemium" model which is commonly practiced by other antivirus vendors outside of China. The difference can be found at several levels. On the surface level, the case study companies offer free fully-functional antivirus software, whereas the "freemium" antivirus vendors usually provide a free edition of their paid-for antivirus software with limited functions. On a deeper level, the revenue model is entirely different. Qihoo 360 and Baidu generate revenue through their online marketing and internet value-added services (VAS) that are offered for enterprises and other business sectors, while, the "freemium" antivirus vendors generate revenue by cross-selling premium products to users. Moreover, for Qihoo 360 and Baidu, the goal is to effectively drive user traffic to support their online advertising service and internet VAS, whereas, for "freemium" antivirus vendors the goal is to convert free users into paying customers.

4. THE MARKET RESEARCH

4.1 Introduction

There are two main objectives of this market research: the first is to find whether the Chinese internet security software vendors' business models can be adopted in the international market. In other words, the study seeks to understand whether the Chinese internet security software vendors can use their business model to achieve similar commercial success in the international market as in the Chinese market. The second is to understand how hard or easy it is for international internet security software vendors to achieve commercial success in the Chinese market, when in direct competition with the Chinese vendors.

To answer these two questions, a comprehensive understanding of both the Chinese and international markets (due to the scope of the study, the international market mainly refers to the Western market, further explained in a later section) is required. Therefore, a market survey questionnaire was applied in order to collect primary data. The data which was collected through the questionnaire is analyzed and presented in this chapter.

4.2 Summary of the data

The questionnaire received 972 valid responses. 34.2% of the responses were from China (including Hong Kong), 33.2 % of responses were from Europe, and 10.5% of the responses were from North America and Australia combined. Among the 972 respondents, male respondents accounted for about 87% of the sample. This could be due to the fact that males are generally more interested in this topic.

A comprehensive data summary report is present in appendix A-2. The detailed analyses of the data are presented in the following sections.

4.3 Comparison analysis

In order to compare the differences and similarities between Chinese and Western users, the data collected by questionnaire will be segmented into two groups: Chinese respondents and Western respondents, according to respondents' geographic location. The Western respondents include European respondents (33.2%), and North American and Australian respondents (10.5%).

The statistics such as average and standard deviation will be calculated from suitable questions, in order to present the normal distribution of the data.

4.3.1   Usage background

In terms of users' usage background, the differences between the two respondent groups are mainly the different choice of operating system, browser, and the type of internet security software employed.

Although both of the two groups indicted a high percentage of using Windows operating systems, however, for Chinese respondents Windows XP still maintains its popularity (30.2%), compared to only 6.4% of the Western respondents who use Windows XP (See Figure 4-1).

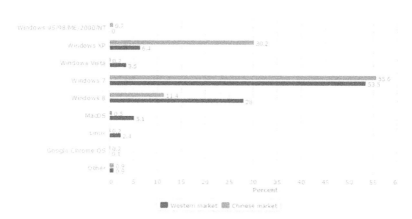

Figure 4-1 Comparison of operating system usage

The greater diversity is distributed by the browser usage, for the western respondents, Mozilla Firefox, Google Chrome, and Microsoft Internet Explorer are the most-used browsers with 46.7%, 36.6%, and 19.2% usage, respectively. For Chinese users, over half of the respondents (52.3%) used Chinese browsers which mainly consist of 360 browser (25.0%) and QQ browser (7.2%) (See Figure 4-2, note, the Chinese browsers are shown as column "Other" in the Figure).

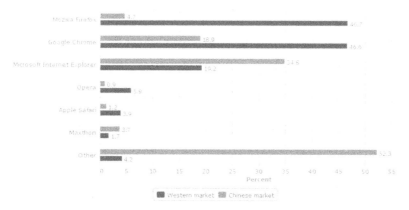

Figure 4-2 Comparison of browser usage

Regarding the current internet security software usage, both of the groups show a similar usage rate, 94.3% of Chinese respondents and 95.0% of Western respondents are currently using security software. 60.3% of Chinese respondents have been victims of cyber-crime, while, for Western respondents this number is 48.9%.

The major difference between the two groups is in the usage of free security software. The Chinese respondents have expressed much higher free security software usage (89.9%) compared to only 39.3% of Western respondents who use free security software (See Figure 4-3).

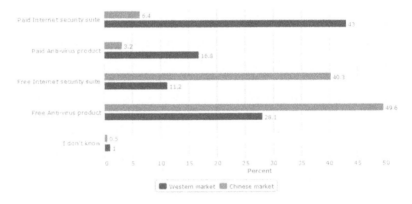

Figure 4-3 Comparison of antivirus software usage

Another main difference is the duration of internet security software user's usage. Most of the Chinese respondents have been using security software for 3 to 5 years (33.6%), or 6 to 10 years (30.4%), while, for Western respondents, over half of them (51.4%) have been using security software more than 10 years (See Figure 4-4).

In order to gain a normal distribution of the data, the questionnaire set numeric reporting values from 1 to 5 to address the opinions "Less than a year" to "More than 10 years" respectively. For Chinese respondents the average number of years was 2.8 which mean between "1 to 3 years" and "4 to 5 years", and the standard deviation is

1.8. For Western respondents the average is 4.1, which means between "5 to 10 years" and "more than 10 years", and the standard deviation is 1.3.

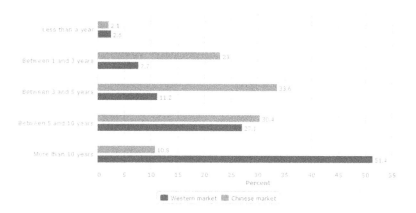

Figure 4-4 Comparison of duration of AV usage

In terms of the expenditure of paid-for security software users, most of the Western respondents (45.3%) spent $28 to $55.99 per year for one PC, while most of the Chinese respondents (38.9%) spent less than $28 per year per PC. However, this does not mean Chinese users of paid-for security software generally spend less; there was a much higher percentage of Chinese respondents (30.6%) who spend $56 to $69.99 per year per PC, compared to Western respondents (11.2%) who spend this amount (See Figure 4-5). For the data of Chinese respondents, the standard deviation was 1.3, whereas for Western respondents the standard deviation was 1.1.

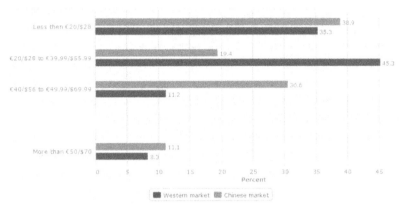

Figure 4-5 Compare annually spending

4.3.2 Consumer behavior

The consumer behavior part of the questionnaire investigated the respondents' buying patterns, the factors influencing buying decisions, and the decision process.

In terms of packaging, over half of the Western respondents (56.7%) prefer downloading security products with electronic documents. Whereas, for Chinese respondents, the boxed product with a CD and printed documents still maintains its popularity with 28.6% of consumers preferring this option. A considerable amount of respondents answered "It doesn't matter for me" for this question for both Chinese respondents and Western respondents with 31.4% and 29.0%, respectively (See Figure 4-6).

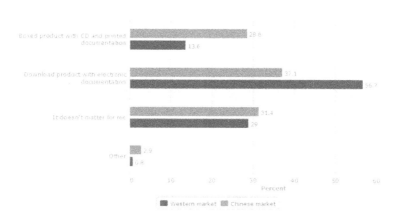

Figure 4-6 Packaging preference

In terms of the place where respondents purchased their security software previously, both respondent groups showed a similar pattern. Although 28.6% of Chinese respondents indicated a preference for the boxed product with CD, the majority of respondents, both Chinese (76.9%) and Western (73.1%), purchased their security software by downloading through the vendor's website (See Figure 4-7).

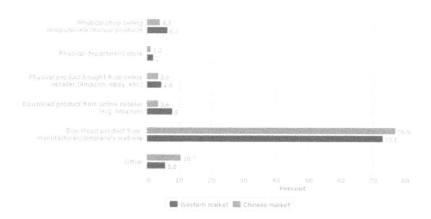

Figure 4-7 Place where respondents got their previous security software

To address the users' decision making process, the questionnaire asked where the respondents would go for advice before choosing security software. The result suggests "Independent AV-testing labs", "expert friend/family members", and "website/search engines" are the three most popular sources of advice for both Chinese and Western respondents. The differences between the two groups are: Chinese respondents more often use "website/search engines" as their information source, while, Western respondents use "online computer magazine", and "Independent AV-testing labs" to get information (See Figure 4-8, note this is a multiple-choice question, therefore the percentage is not relevant).

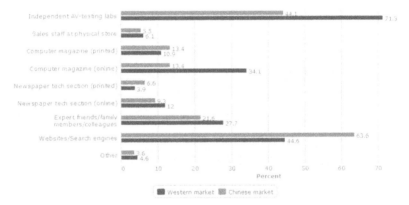

Figure 4-8 Sources of advice for security software

The main difference here is that, when asked about how often the respondents read reviews/test reports of security software, most of the Chinese respondents indicated "Rarely" (26.7%) or "Sometimes" (32.5%), while, most of the Western respondents indicated "Often" (30.2%) or "Always" (42.1%) (See Figure 4-9).

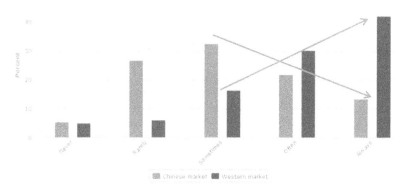

Figure 4-9 How often the respondents read reviews/test reports of security software

4.3.3 Attitude

Both Western and Chinese respondents indicated similar opinions regarding the "protection against malware", where both groups perceive that paid-for security software denotes a better production (See Figure 4-10).

Protection against malware

Segment		Paid software	Free software
Chinese market	Average	★ ★ ★ ★ ☆ 4.17	★ ★ ★ ★ 3.69
Western market	Average	★ ★ ★ ★ ☆ 4.40	★ ★ ★ ★ 3.52

Figure 4-10 Protection against malware

Although, both Chinese and Western respondents believe paid-for security software offers better technical support, Chinese respondents perceive that there was little difference between free and paid-for security software, while Western respondents perceive that the free security software is of a much poorer quality than the paid-for security software on technical support (See Figure 4-11).

Technical support

Segment		Paid software	Free software
Chinese market	Average	★★★★✩ 4.22	★★★★✩ 3.54
Western market	Average	★★★★✩ 4.31	★★✩✩✩ 2.38

Figure 4-11 Technical support

Compared to the Chinese respondents, Western respondents expressed more concern about the privacy issues regarding the free security software (See Figure 4-12).

Privacy of my data

Segment		Paid software	Free software
Chinese market	Average	★★★★✩ 4.13	★★★★✩ 3.51
Western market	Average	★★★★✩ 4.14	★★★✩✩ 3.06

Figure 4-12 Privacy of my data

In terms of "user friendliness", the Chinese respondents perceived that free security software is more easy to use than paid-for security software, which is exactly opposite to the Western respondents' opinion (See Figure 4-13).

Ease of use

Segment		Paid software	Free software
Chinese market	Average	★★★★✩ 3.67	★★★★★ 4.24
Western market	Average	★★★★✩ 4.03	★★★★✩ 3.91

Figure 4-13 User friendliness

A significant difference in opinion occurred when the two groups were asked their perception of the number of features of the free and paid-for security software. The Chinese respondents perceived that the free security software had more features than the paid-for security software, while the Western respondents perceived that the free security software had much fewer features than the paid-for security software (See Figure 4-14).

Number of features

Segment		Paid software	Free software
Chinese market	Average	★ ★ ★ ★ 3.77	★ ★ ★ ★ ☆ 4.07
Western market	Average	★ ★ ★ ★ ☆ 4.45	★ ★ ★ 2.96

Figure 4-14 Number of features

To address the country-of-origin effect (COE), the questionnaire provided seven selected countries (Russia, China, USA, Germany, Romania, Czech Republic, and Finland) for respondents to rate on a scale from -3 to +3, where -3 indicates an extremely negative image, while +3 indicate an extremely positive image.

Over half of the Chinese respondents (57.0%) and nearly half of the Western respondents (49.1%) would consider the product's country-of-origin when choosing security software. Chinese respondents indicated a very positive country image associated with China, the USA, and Germany (see figure 4-15) while, Western respondents expressed a very positive image towards Germany, the USA, and Finland. A noticeable difference was that Western respondents expressed a very strong negative associated country image towards China (See Figure 4-16).

	-3 Extremely negative		-2		-1		0		+1		+2		+3 Extremely positive		Responses
Russia	11	6.9%	4	2.5%	8	5.0%	44	27.5%	29	18.1%	37	23.1%	27	16.9%	160
China	7	3.9%	7	3.9%	11	6.2%	26	14.6%	29	16.3%	35	19.7%	63	35.4%	178
USA	21	13.0%	4	2.5%	6	3.7%	34	21.1%	30	18.6%	32	19.9%	34	21.1%	161
Germany	12	7.7%	3	1.9%	4	2.6%	45	28.8%	27	17.3%	28	17.9%	37	23.7%	156
Romania	15	9.7%	6	3.9%	6	3.9%	77	50.0%	20	13.0%	16	10.4%	14	9.1%	154
Czech Republic	13	8.4%	6	3.9%	5	3.2%	67	43.5%	23	14.9%	23	14.9%	17	11.0%	154
Finland	14	9.2%	6	3.9%	6	3.9%	64	42.1%	30	19.7%	16	10.5%	16	10.5%	152

Figure 4-15 Chinese respondents on COE

	-3 Extremely negative		-2		-1		0		+1		+2		+3 Extremely positive		Responses
Russia	44	15.2%	33	11.4%	38	12.4%	40	13.8%	46	15.9%	42	14.5%	49	16.9%	290
China	103	35.5%	63	21.7%	42	14.5%	53	18.3%	19	6.6%	5	1.7%	5	1.7%	290
USA	27	9.3%	22	7.6%	20	6.9%	39	13.4%	45	15.5%	70	24.1%	68	23.4%	291
Germany	1	0.3%	0	0.0%	2	0.7%	37	12.7%	49	16.8%	101	34.7%	101	34.7%	291
Romania	35	12.2%	29	10.1%	34	11.8%	91	31.7%	40	13.9%	41	14.3%	17	5.9%	287
Czech Republic	18	6.2%	18	6.2%	25	8.7%	91	31.5%	55	19.0%	60	20.8%	22	7.6%	289
Finland	3	1.0%	2	0.7%	4	1.4%	81	27.9%	61	21.0%	77	26.6%	62	21.4%	290

Figure 4-16 Western respondents on COE

4.3.4 Future usage intention

This part of the questionnaire focused on investigating the respondents' intention to use free or paid-for security software in the future.

When asked "are you considering changing your current security software?" both groups showed similar results, as 18.3% of Chinese respondents and 23.0% of Western respondents indicated their intention to change their current security software, and out of these, only 9.4% of the Chinese respondents would change to paid-for security software compared to 20.0% of Western respondents who would change to paid-for security software.

"Poor protection against malware" is the main reason for respondents' intention to change their current security software, both for Chinese respondents (46.4%) and Western respondents (39.0%). For Chinese respondents the other top reasons are "not easy to use" (30.4%) and "Bad reputation of the company" (23.2%). For Western respondents, 44.9% of them indicate "Other reasons", which are mainly "slows the computer performance" or "similar product available for free" (See Figure 4-17).

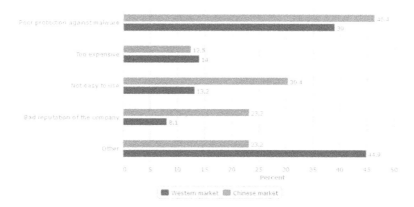

Figure 4-17 The main reasons for changing security software

4.3.5 Mobile security software usage

Android OS is the most commonly used mobile operating system, both for Chinese respondents (70.4%) and Western respondents (55.1%), followed by IOS (apple), with 12.7% usage from Chinese respondents and 16.8% from Western respondents. A noticeable difference is that 15.1% of Western respondents do not use a smart phone, while, this number is only 6.6% for Chinese respondents (See Figure 4-18).

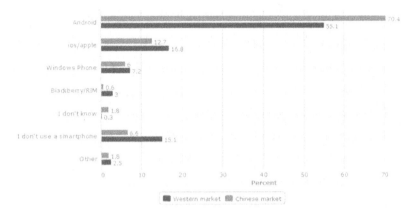

Figure 4-18 Smart phone usage

The major difference is in mobile security software usage. More than two-thirds of Chinese respondents (69.2%) currently use a mobile security app, while, only 40.9% of Western respondents used a mobile security app.

In terms of the type of mobile security software, the majority of Chinese respondents (96.5%) used a free mobile security app. Only 64.1% of Western respondents used a free mobile security app.

4.4 Cross tab analysis

The purpose of cross tab analysis is to investigate the factors which influence the respondents' security software choice (free/paid-for). Due to the purpose of this analysis, the respondents were analyzed as a whole without segmentation.

The cross tab analysis was employed to examine the relationship between users' choice of security software and the factors affecting this such as users' computing habits, demographic background, past experience, and consumer behavior.

4.4.1 Computing habits and users' choice of security software

In order to measure the users' computing habits, the respondents were asked to indicate how frequently they used a computer for the following activities: entertainment, work/business, study/research, electronic banking, online shopping, and downloading. The purpose of this section is to investigate if there is a significant correlation between those activities and the users' choice of security software (free/paid-for). The significance level was set at 0.05 (5%), therefore if the p-value was found to be less than 0.05, the result would be considered statistically significant.

The result shows that there is no significant correlation between users' choice of security software and the user activities of entertainment, work/business, and study/research, as the p-value was 0.4856 (>0.05), 0.3836 (> 0.05), and 0.9426 (> 0.05), respectively. However, the analysis does suggest a strong correlation between users' choice of security software and the activities of electronic banking, online shopping, and downloading, with the p-Value equal to 0.0000 (< 0.05), 0.0147 (< 0.05), and 0.0012 (< 0.05), respectively.

The results shown in figure 4-19, which demonstrate how frequently the respondents use electronic banking, have a strong correlation with their choice of security software. The more frequently the user practices electronic banking the more likely he/she uses paid-for security software. On the other hand, the less frequently a user practices electronic banking, the more likely he/she uses free security software (See Figure 4-19). Online shopping indicated a similar pattern; the more respondents participated in online shipping, the more likely they were to use paid-for security software, and vice versa (See Figure 4-19).

For downloading, the pattern is not as clear for electronic banking and Online shopping, however the statistical results imply that there is a significant correlation (p-Value =0.0012) between downloading and users' choice of security software.

What kind of security software are you using?

Electronic banking (e.g. paying bills, viewing statements, transferring funds)

	At least once a day	At least once a week	At least once a month	Less than once a month	Never	Total
Paid Internet security suite	71 41.7%	120 33.7%	52 28.3%	18 22.8%	21 25.3%	282
Paid Anti-virus product	22 14.6%	58 16.3%	14 7.6%	5 6.3%	8 9.6%	107
Free Internet security suite	26 17.4%	65 18.3%	49 26.6%	21 26.6%	17 20.5%	178
Free Anti-virus product	29 19.5%	109 30.6%	69 37.5%	34 43.0%	37 44.6%	278

Online shopping

	At least once a day	At least once a week	At least once a month	Less than once a month	Never	Total
Paid Internet security suite	31 40.8%	84 37.3%	102 33.9%	54 27.7%	15 23.1%	286
Paid Anti-virus product	9 11.8%	31 13.8%	43 14.3%	22 11.3%	2 3.1%	107
Free Internet security suite	20 26.3%	42 18.7%	61 20.3%	45 23.1%	13 20.0%	181
Free Anti-virus product	15 19.7%	66 29.3%	93 30.9%	73 37.4%	35 53.8%	282

Downloading

	At least once a day	At least once a week	At least once a month	Less than once a month	Never	Total
Paid Internet security suite	160 40.2%	96 27.5%	25 25.0%	11 20.8%	3 42.9%	285
Paid Anti-virus product	45 11.3%	32 10.2%	20 20.0%	10 18.9%	1 14.3%	106
Free Internet security suite	89 22.4%	69 22.0%	16 16.0%	10 18.9%	1 14.3%	185
Free Anti-virus product	102 25.6%	125 39.9%	38 38.0%	21 39.6%	2 28.6%	288

Figure 4-19 The correlation between computing activities and users' choice of security software

4.4.2   Demographic factors and users' choice of security software

In this section the demographic factors are analyzed in order to investigate the correlation between respondents' demographic background and their choice of security software (free/paid-for). The demographic factors include educational level, occupation, and monthly income.

The statistical results suggest that the correlation between education level and the choice of security software is not statistically significant, as the p-Value = 0.0642(> 0.05). The occupation and monthly income have a significant correlation towards users' choice of security software, with p-Value equal to 0.0000 and 0.0004, respectively.

In terms of occupation, the results suggest that the respondents of the following occupations: Executive/Managerial, Computer Technical/Engineering, and retired, have a particularly high percentage of using paid-for security software, whereas, the respondents, including: College/Graduate Students, Academic/Educator, and Sales/Marketing, have a high percentage of using free security software. This result can be partly explained by the income analysis presented in the following section.

The income level has a straightforward correlation with the users' choice of security software, where the higher the respondents' income was, the more likely they are to use paid-for security software, and vice versa (See Figure 4-20).

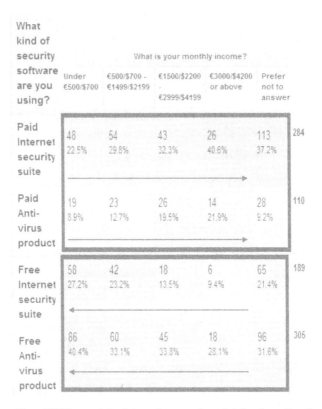

What kind of security software are you using?	What is your monthly income?				
	Under €500/$700	€500/$700 - €1499/$2199	€1500/$2200 - €2999/$4199	€3000/$4200 or above	Prefer not to answer
Paid Internet security suite	48 22.5%	54 29.8%	43 32.3%	26 40.6%	113 37.2%	284
Paid Anti-virus product	19 8.9%	23 12.7%	26 19.5%	14 21.9%	28 9.2%	110
Free Internet security suite	58 27.2%	42 23.2%	18 13.5%	6 9.4%	65 21.4%	189
Free Anti-virus product	86 40.4%	60 33.1%	45 33.8%	18 28.1%	96 31.6%	305

Figure 4-20 The correlation between income and users' choice of security software

4.4.3   Users' past experience and users' choice of security software

The users' past experiences includes two factors: the experience of being victims of cyber-crime, and the duration of security software usage (how long respondents have been using security software). Both of the factors have been found to be statistically significant with the p-Value equal to 0.0397, and 0.0000, respectively.

Although there is a significant correlation between experience of being victims of cyber-crime and the choice of security software, the pattern of this relationship may be very different from the common expectation. The results suggest that the respondents who have been victims of cyber-crime actually have a slightly higher percentage of using the free security software (58.8%). This may be due to the sampling error (p = 0.0397), for which there is a higher percentage of students (19.5%) and computer technicians (19.5%) in the sample. However, the results can still imply that the experience of being a victim of cyber-crime does not strongly affect users' choice of security software (See Figure 4-21).

In terms of security software usage duration, the results suggest the duration that respondents have been using security software is a good predictor of what kind of security software they use. Basically the longer the respondents have been using security software, the more likely they are to use paid-for security software, and vice versa (See Figure 4-21).

Have you ever been the victim of any kind of cyber crime (e.g. malware infection or hacker attack), or lost personal data (e.g. by hard disk failure)?

What kind of security software are you using?	Yes	No	Total		How long have you been using security software?					
					Less than a year	Between 1 and 3 years	Between 3 and 5 years	Between 5 and 10 years	More than 10 years	Total
Paid Internet security suite	135 27.6%	153 37.3%	289		3 16.7%	14 13.5%	43 24.9%	77 30.0%	153 43.2%	290
Paid Anti-virus product	63 12.8%	46 11.2%	109		1 5.6%	11 10.6%	9 5.2%	27 10.5%	62 17.5%	110
Free Internet security suite	114 23.2%	76 18.5%	190		3 16.7%	26 25.0%	49 28.3%	49 19.1%	63 17.8%	190
Free Anti-virus product	175 35.6%	132 32.2%	307		10 55.6%	52 50.0%	71 41.0%	102 39.7%	74 20.9%	309
I don't know	4 0.8%	3 0.7%	7		1 5.6%	1 1.0%	1 0.6%	2 0.8%	2 0.6%	7
Totals	492 100%	410 100%	902		18	104	173	257	354	906

Figure 4-21 The correlation between past experiences and users' choice of security software

4.4.4   Consumer behavior factors and users' choice of security software

In this final section, the research analyzed the correlation between consumer behavior and the users' choice of security software. The statistical results suggested that factors such as the frequency of reading reviews/test reports and the sources of advice have a strong statistically significant correlation to users' choice of security software, with P-Value equal to 0.0000, for both factors.

How often the respondents read reviews/test reports has a clear relation to users' choice of security software. The results indicated that the respondents who "always" read reviews/test reports of security software have a higher percentage of having used paid-for security software (61.5%). Whereas, 66.7% of respondents who "never" read reviews/test reports typically use free security software (See Figure 4-22).

In terms of the source of advice, the respondents who tend to get advice from online newspapers, friends/family/colleagues, and Websites/Search engines, are more likely to use free security software. The respondents who tend to get advice from, independent AV-testing labs, sales staff at a physical store, and computer magazine (printed/online), are more likely to use paid-for security software (See Figure 4-22).

What kind of security software are you using?	If you wanted to buy a new security product, where would you go for advice?										How often do you read reviews/test reports before you choose security products?					
	Independent AV-testing labs	Sales staff at physical store	Computer magazine (printed)	Computer magazine (online)	Newspaper tech section (printed)	Newspaper tech section (online)	Expert friends/family members/colleagues	Websites/Search engines	Other	Total	Never	Rarely	Sometimes	Often	Always	Total
Paid Internet security suite	236 40.8%	18 39.1%	48 44.4%	111 44.0%	19 42.2%	36 37.1%	60 29.9%	132 23.1%	19 45.3%	679	3 8.3%	10 8.5%	40 20.2%	88 35.9%	149 49.0%	290
Paid Anti-virus product	75 13.0%	6 13.0%	10 9.3%	27 10.7%	3 6.7%	10 10.3%	27 12.1%	49 10.4%	7 17.1%	214	8 22.2%	7 6.0%	25 12.6%	31 12.7%	38 12.5%	109
Free Internet security suite	119 20.6%	7 15.2%	27 25.0%	44 17.5%	10 22.2%	21 21.6%	43 19.3%	112 23.9%	3 7.3%	386	6 16.7%	37 31.6%	60 30.3%	43 17.6%	43 14.1%	189
Free Anti-virus product	147 25.4%	15 32.6%	23 21.3%	70 27.8%	13 28.9%	30 30.9%	88 39.5%	176 37.5%	11 26.8%	573	18 50.0%	60 51.3%	71 35.9%	83 33.9%	73 24.0%	305
I don't know	1 0.2%	0 0.0%	0 0.0%	0 0.0%	0 0.0%	0 0.0%	5 2.2%	0 0.0%	1 2.4%	7	1 2.8%	3 2.6%	2 1.0%	0 0.0%	1 0.3%	7
Totals	578 100%	46 100%	108 100%	252 100%	45 100%	97 100%	223 100%	469 100%	41 100%	1859	36 100%	117 100%	198 100%	245 100%	304 100%	900

Figure 4-22 The correlation between consumer behavior factors and users' choice of security software

4.5 Discussion

In this section, the primary data that was collected through the questionnaire has been analyzed with comparison analysis and cross tab analysis. The comparison analysis compared Chinese respondents and Western respondents from the perspective of the user's knowledge of security software, consumer behavior, attitude, future usage intention, and mobile security software usage. The cross tab analysis examined the correlation between users' choice of security software and factors such as users' computing habit, demographic background, experience, and consumer behavior.

In terms of comparison analysis, the results suggested many differences between Chinese and Western respondents, especially in relation to consumer behavior and their attitude towards security software. Chinese respondents have expressed a much higher free security software usage (89.9%) compared to only 39.3% of Western respondents who use free security software. Most of the Western respondents (45.3%) spend $28 to $55.99 per year for one PC, while most Chinese respondents (38.9%) spend less than $28 per year per PC. Chinese respondents more often use "website/search engines" as their source of information, while Western respondents are more likely to use online computer magazines and Independent AV-testing labs to get information. Over half of the Chinese respondents (57%) and nearly half of the Western respondents (49.1%) would consider the product's country-of-origin when choosing security software. In this case, the Chinese respondents showed a positive country image towards China, USA, and Germany (see Figure 4-15), while the Western respondent expressed a strong negatively associated country image towards China (see Figure 4-16).

To sum up, the PC security market is a relatively new market for China in comparison to the West. Paid-for security software does not have a strong base in the Chinese retail market. This created a suitable market environment for free security software to thrive in the Chinese market. Compared with the relatively "young" PC security market, China has a more matured mobile security market, as there is a higher percentage of smart phone users and a higher usage of mobile security software than the West.

In terms of cross-tab analysis, the results show that the respondents who are retired or who work in Executive/Managerial or Computer Technical/Engineering positions, have a high percentage of using paid security software. The respondents, who are College/Graduate Student, Academic/Educator, or work as Sales/Marketing, have a high percentage of using free security software.

Users' computing habits can also indicate their choice of security software. The users who often use electronic banking are more likely to use paid-for security software. Online shopping indicated a similar pattern; the more respondents participate in online shopping, the more likely they are to use paid-for security software. The same pattern is also found in the respondents' income level, the higher the respondents' income the more likely they are to use paid-for security software, and vice versa.

In terms of the consumer behavior, the respondents who tend to get advice from "online newspapers", "friends/family/colleagues", and "Websites/Search engines", are more likely to use free security software. Respondents, who tend to get advice from, "Independent AV-testing labs", "Sales staff at physical store", and "Computer magazine (printed/online)", are more likely to use paid-for security software.

5. SUMMARY AND CONCLUSION

5.1 Brief summary of this study

The aim of this study is to investigate the business model of Chinese "free" antivirus software vendors and to analyze the Chinese Internet security market.

The study analyzed the business model of two selected Chinese AV-vendors, Qihoo 360 and Baidu, in relation to product development, revenue, marketing and distribution, and services and implementation models. In addition, a market research was conducted to compare the Chinese and Western users, and to examine the influential factors on users' choice of security software.

5.2 Conclusion

Anderson believes that "every industry that becomes digital, eventually becomes free" (Anderson, 2006). The story of Qihoo 360 and Baidu in this research shows how a digital product eventually becomes free and how the companies make a profit from it. Taking Qihoo 360 as an example, the company uses its free Internet security software to generate their user base, and uses a series of channel products such as browser and desktop app, to transform the user base into user traffic. With the established user traffic, Qihoo 360 adopted an advertising revenue model by developing a series of platform products and web services. Through the advertising and internet VAS, Qihoo 360 generated enough revenue to support its free internet security products.

However, it is still too early to say that "free" is the future of the antivirus industry. The "free" model practiced by Qihoo 360 and Baidu needs various supporting and implementing processes to achieve commercial success. It is hard for a traditional software company to build the necessary elements to adopt this model, and it is also difficult for Qihoo 360 and Baidu to achieve commercial value with this model in the overseas markets. Especially, when considering the Western market, the more matured internet regulations make it more different for the case study companies to drive user traffic.

For the mobile security market, the study shows that compared to the Western market, China has a higher percentage of smart phone users and a higher usage of mobile security software. This may be due to the lower penetration rate of the PC in China compared to the West. Due to the large user traffic potential from mobile devices, it can be expected that in the future Chinese free security software vendors will focus more on the mobile security market.

For international AV-vendors, this study has shown that it is difficult to compete with Chinese free security software vendors in the Chinese market on home users, because of the well-established user base of these companies. However, market research also found that there are market opportunities for high-end users in China, where people spend more than $56 annually per PC (see Chapter 4). In addition, because the volume of user traffic is the key to the "free" model, the Chinese free AV-vendors may take less interest in corporate users. Therefore, focusing on corporate users could be an effective strategy for international AV-vendors to establish a presence in the Chinese market.

5.3 Limitations

The representativeness of market research is limited. The male respondents accounted for about 87% of the sample. Therefore, the results of the market survey are not generalized to the entire population of internet security users. Additionally, the raw data generated from the market survey can be further analyzed in future study to increase the contribution to the literature.

BIBLIOGRAPHY

About sungy mobile. (n.d.). *Sungy mobile*. Retrieved July 27, 2014, from

http://www.sungymobile.com/about.html

Alt, R., & Zimmermann, H.-D. (2007). *Introduction to Special Section - Business*

Models (SSRN Scholarly Paper No. ID 1018067). Rochester, NY: Social

Science   Research   Network.   Retrieved   from

http://papers.ssrn.com/abstract=1018067

Baidu   Inc.   ADS.   (n.d.).   Retrieved   June   22,   2014,   from

http://www.marketwatch.com/investing/stock/bidu

Baidu Promote, pricing. (n.d.). *Baidu Promote*. Retrieved June 24, 2014, from

http://e.baidu.com/product/searchpro/tgfy/

Baidu releases cheap smartphone. (n.d.). *BBC News*. Retrieved June 22, 2014, from

http://www.bbc.co.uk/news/technology-18069498

Baidu, Inc. (n.d.). *Baidu Announces First Quarter 2014 Results*. Retrieved June 22,

2014,   from

http://ir.baidu.com/phoenix.zhtml?c=188488&p=irol-newsArticle&ID=19222

19&highlight=

Brandenburger, A. M., & Stuart, H. W. (1996). Value-based Business Strategy.

Journal of Economics & Management Strategy, *5*(1), 5–24.

CCID Consulting. (2014a). *Business logic behind Qihoo 360*. Retrieved from

http://www.ccidconsulting.com/glpl/3321.jhtml

CCID Consulting. (2014b). *Market research report of China corporate/enterprise antivirus products.* Retrieved from http://www.ccidconsulting.com/u/cms/www/201404/01150904bccv.pdf

China Search Engine Market Reached 11.16 Bn Yuan in Q1 2014. (n.d.). *China Internet Watch.* Retrieved June 22, 2014, from http://www.chinainternetwatch.com/7375/china-search-engine-market-q1-201 4/

China Stock Research - Baidu Inc. (BIDU). (n.d.). Retrieved June 22, 2014, from http://www.chinastockresearch.com/company-profiles/item/401-baidu-inc-bid u.html?highlight=WyJiYWlkdSJd

China Stock Research - Qihoo 360 Technologies (QIHU). (n.d.). Retrieved June 18, 2014, from http://www.chinastockresearch.com/company-profiles/company-summaries/it em/215-qihoo-360-technologies-qihu/215-qihoo-360-technologies-qihu.html

Comes, S., & Berniker, L. (2008). Business Model Innovation. In D. D. Pantaleo & N. Pal (Eds.), *From Strategy to Execution* (pp. 65–86). Springer Berlin Heidelberg. Retrieved from http://link.springer.com/chapter/10.1007/978-3-540-71880-2_4

Giesen, E., Berman, S. J., Bell, R., & Blitz, A. (2007). Three ways to successfully innovate your business model. *Strategy & Leadership, 35*(6), 27–33.

Google Inc. (2014). *Storage plan pricing. Storage plan pricing.* Retrieved from https://support.google.com/drive/answer/2375123?hl=en

Granstrand, O. (2005). Innovation and intellectual property rights. *The Oxford Handbook of Innovation*, 266–290.

History and Milestones. (n.d.). *Investor Relations of Qihoo 360*. Retrieved July 27, 2014, from http://ir.360.cn/frame.zhtml?c=243376&p=irol-govHistoryMilestones

IDF Laboratory. (2012). *Independent Report on Alledged "Hidden Backdoor" in Qihoo 360 Secure Browser*. Retrieved from http://www.valleytalk.org/wp-content/uploads/2013/03/Independent-Report-o n-Alledged-Hidden-Backdoor-in-Qihoo-360-Secure-Browser-v1.4.pdf

Investor relationship, products. (2014, June 22). *Baidu Investors relationship*. Retrieved from http://ir.baidu.com/phoenix.zhtml?c=188488&p=irol-products

Iresearch. (2010). Retrieved January 23, 2014, from http://news.imeigu.com/a/1301297991113.html

Jane McEntegart. (2011). *The $79 Kindle Costs Amazon $84 to Make. Tom's Hardware*. Retrieved May 9, 2014, from http://www.tomshardware.com/news/Amazon-Kindle-Cost-Production-Suppl ies-Parts,13953.html

Johnson, M. W., Christensen, C. M., & Kagermann, H. (2008). Reinventing your business model. *Harvard Business Review, 86*(12), 57–68.

Klein, S., & Loebbecke, C. (2000). The transformation of pricing models on the web:

examples from the airline industry. In *13th International Bled Electronic Commerce Conference* (pp. 19–21). Retrieved from http://www.mm.uni-koeln.de/team-loebbecke-publications-conf-proceedings/ Conf-045-2000-The%20Transformation%20of%20Pricing%20Models.pdf

Lina Wang. (2010, July 2). Qihoo 360 rise lawsuit against Rising. *Beijing Times*. Retrieved from http://tech.xinmin.cn/2010/07/02/5542072.html

Morris, M., Schindehutte, M., & Allen, J. (2005). The entrepreneur's business model: toward a unified perspective. *Journal of Business Research, 58*(6), 726–735.

Osterwalder, A., & Pigneur, Y. (2002a). An e-business model ontology for modeling e-business. In *15th Bled electronic commerce conference* (pp. 17–19). Bled, Slovenia. Retrieved from http://student.bus.olemiss.edu/files/conlon/Others/Others/__BookChapter_So cialMEsia_EBusiness/An%20e-Business%20Model%20Ontology%20for%2 0Modeling%20e-Business.pdf

Osterwalder, A., & Pigneur, Y. (2002b). Business models and their elements. In *Position paper for the international workshop on business models, Lausanne, Switzerland.* Retrieved from http://inforge.unil.ch/aosterwa/Documents/workshop/Osterwalder_Pigneur.pd f

Osterwalder, A., & Pigneur, Y. (2010). *Business model generation: a handbook for visionaries, game changers, and challengers.* John Wiley & Sons. Pateli, A.,

& Giaglis, G. M. (2003). A framework for understanding and analysing e-business models. In *Bled Electronic Commerce Conference* (Vol. 2003). Citeseer. Retrieved from http://citeseerx.ist.psu.edu/viewdoc/download?doi=10.1.1.198.7354&rep=rep 1&type=pdf

Product&Service. (n.d.). *Investor Relations of Qihoo 360*. Retrieved June 18, 2014, from http://corp.360.cn/ps/overview.html

Qihoo 360 Reports First Quarter 2014 Unaudited Financial Results. (n.d.). *Yahoo Finance*. Retrieved June 5, 2014, from http://finance.yahoo.com/news/qihoo-360-reports-first-quarter-220000519.ht ml

Qihoo 360 Technology Co. Ltd. (n.d.). *History and Milestones*. Retrieved June 18, 2014, from http://ir.360.cn/frame.zhtml?c=243376&p=irol-govHistoryMilestones

Qihoo 360 Technology Co. Ltd, n.d. (n.d.). *Financial Reports. Investor Relations of Qihoo 360*. Retrieved June 18, 2014, from http://ir.360.cn/phoenix.zhtml?c=243376&p=irol-reportsannual

Qihoo 360 Technology Co. Ltd. (n.d.). *Qihoo 360 Reports Fourth Quarter and Fiscal Year 2013 Unaudited Financial Results. Press release*. Retrieved June 18, 2014, from http://ir.360.cn/phoenix.zhtml?c=243376&p=irol-newsArticle&ID=1907039

&highlight=

Qihoo 360 Technology Co. Ltd. Marketing platform. (n.d.). *360 marketing platform.*

Retrieved   June   21,   2014,   from

http://e.360.cn/static/help/list.html?n=1-2-1&8143657320179045

Qihoo 360 Technology Co. Ltd. Open platform. (n.d.). *360 open platform.* Retrieved

from http://dev.360.cn/dev/policy

Qihoo 360 Technology Co.,Ltd., marketing platform. (n.d.). *Market news.* Retrieved

June 20, 2014, from http://e.360.cn/static/news/

Rajala, R., Rossi, M., & Tuunainen, V. K. (2003). A framework for analyzing

software business models. In *ECIS* (pp. 1614–1627). Retrieved from

http://sdaw.info/asp/aspecis/20030126.pdf

Shafer, S. M., Smith, H. J., & Linder, J. C. (2005). The power of business models.

Business Horizons, 48(3), 199–207.

Sun, P. (2014). Study on the connotation, cause and overtake strategy across in the

operation of enterprise micro-innovation business model: A case research on

Jihu 360. *Journal of Chemical and Pharmaceutical Research, 6*(1), 1–6.

Teece, D. J. (2010). Business models, business strategy and innovation. *Long Range

Planning, 43*(2), 172–194.

Top internet companies: global market value 2014 | Statistic. (n.d.). *Statista.*

Retrieved   June   22,   2014,   from

http://www.statista.com/statistics/277483/market-value-of-the-largest-internet

-companies-worldwide/

Wholey, J. S. (1979). *Evaluation.*

Wilson, F. (2006). The freemium business model. *A VC Blog, March, 23.*

Yin, R. K. (2009). *Case Study Research: Design and Methods.* SAGE.

Zott, C., & Amit, R. (2010). Business model design: an activity system perspective.

Long Range Planning, 43(2), 216–226.

LIST OF APPENDICES

Appendix A-1 Questionnaire

Market survey of Internet security software

Page description:
Thank you very much for participating in my survey. Firstly, we would like to ask you a few questions about your computing background.

1. Which operating system do you mainly use?

- ◯ Windows 95/98/ME/2000/NT
- ◯ Windows XP
- ◯ Windows Vista
- ◯ Windows 7
- ◯ Windows 8
- ◯ MacOS
- ◯ Linux
- ◯ Google Chrome OS
- ◯ Other [　　　　　　　]

2. Which web browser do you mainly use?

- ☐ Mozilla Firefox
- ☐ Apple Safari
- ☐ Opera
- ☐ Google Chrome
- ☐ Microsoft Internet Explorer
- ☐ Maxthon
- ☐ Other [　　　　　　　]

3. How would you describe your level of computer proficiency?

- ○ Elementary User
- ○ Intermediate User
- ○ Proficient User
- ○ Enthusiast
- ○ IT Professional
- ○ I don't know

4. How frequently do you use a PC for the following activities?

	At least once a day	At least once a week	At least once a month	Less than once a month	Never
Entertainment (e. g. media, gaming, internet surfing, social networks)	○	○	○	○	○
Work/business	○	○	○	○	○
Study/research	○	○	○	○	○
Electronic banking (e. g. paying bills, viewing statements, transferring funds)	○	○	○	○	○
Online shopping	○	○	○	○	○
Downloading	○	○	○	○	○

5. Are you currently using security software?

- ○ Yes
- ○ No

6. Have you ever been the victim of any kind of cyber-crime (e.g. malware infection or hacker attack), or lost personal data (e.g. by hard-disk failure)?

- ○ Yes
- ○ No

Logic Hidden unless: Question "Are you currently using security software?" #5 contains any ("Yes")

7. How long have you been using security software?

- Less than a year
- Between 1 and 3 years
- Between 3 and 5 years
- Between 5 and 10 years
- More than 10 years

Logic Hidden unless: Question "Are you currently using security software?" #5 contains any ("Yes")

8. What kind of security software are you using?

- Paid Internet security suite
- Paid Anti-virus product
- Free Internet security suite
- Free Anti-virus product
- I don't know

Logic Hidden unless: Question "What kind of security software are you using?" #8 contains any ("Paid Internet security suite","Paid Anti-virus product")

9. How much do you spend per computer on security software annually?

- Less then €20/$28
- €20/$28 to €39.99/$55.99
- €40/$56 to €49.99/$69.99
- More than €50/$70

LOGIC Hidden unless: Question "What kind of security software are you using?" #8 contains any ("Paid Internet security suite","Paid Anti-virus product")
10. Did you know that free antivirus products are available?

○ Yes

○ No

LOGIC Hidden unless: Question "Are you currently using security software?" #5 contains any ("No")
11. Do you intend to start using security software in the near future?

○ Yes

○ No

○ Not sure

Section B: Buying behavior B-1

LOGIC Hidden unless: (Question "What kind of security software are you using?" #8 contains any ("Paid Internet security suite","Paid Anti-virus product") AND Question "Did you know that free antivirus products are available?" #10 contains any ("Yes"))
12. Why do you prefer to pay for security software rather than use a free program?

☐ I don't think free programs are as good as paid-for programs

☐ I believe there have better technical support if I pay for the software

☐ The product I prefer to use is not available for free

☐ I believe Free products will display too many nag screens and advertising

☐ Other [＿＿＿＿＿]

LOGIC Hidden unless: Question "What kind of security software are you using?" #8 contains any ("Paid Internet security suite","Paid Anti-virus product")
13. When you buying a security software, what kind of packaging do you prefer?

○ Boxed product with CD and printed documentation

○ Download product with electronic documentation

○ It doesn't matter for me

○ Other [＿＿＿＿＿]

Logic Hidden unless: Question "Are you currently using security software?" #5 contains any ("Yes")

14. Where did you get your security software last time?

- ○ Physical shop selling computer/electronics products
- ○ Physical department store
- ○ Physical product bought from online retailer (Amazon, eBay, etc.)
- ○ Download product from online retailer (e.g. Amazon)
- ○ Download product from manufacturer/company's website
- ○ Other [_____]

15. If you wanted to buy a new security product, where would you go for advice?

- ☐ Computer magazine (online)
- ☐ Computer magazine (printed)
- ☐ Newspaper tech section (printed)
- ☐ Newspaper tech section (online)
- ☐ Websites/Search engines
- ☐ Expert friends/family members/colleagues
- ☐ Sales staff at physical store
- ☐ Independent AV-testing labs
- ☐ Other [_____]

16. How often do you read reviews/test reports before you choose security products?

Never	Rarely	Sometimes	Often	Always
○	○	○	○	○

17. How important are the following factors on your choice of security software?

	Not at all important	Not important	Neutral	Important	Very important	Not Applicable
Price	○	○	○	○	○	○
Protection from malware	○	○	○	○	○	○
Ease of installation	○	○	○	○	○	○
Ease of use	○	○	○	○	○	○
Number of features	○	○	○	○	○	○
Performance (impact on system speed)	○	○	○	○	○	○

Section C: Attitude towards security software C-1

18. In your opinion, how well do you think free security software compares with paid-for products?

5 star = extremely good. 1 star = extremely bad

	Paid security software	Free of charge security software
Protection against malware	○ ☆ ☆ ☆ ☆ ☆	○ ☆ ☆ ☆ ☆ ☆
Privacy of my data	○ ☆ ☆ ☆ ☆ ☆	○ ☆ ☆ ☆ ☆ ☆
Ease of use	○ ☆ ☆ ☆ ☆ ☆	○ ☆ ☆ ☆ ☆ ☆
Number of features	○ ☆ ☆ ☆ ☆ ☆	○ ☆ ☆ ☆ ☆ ☆
Technical support	○ ☆ ☆ ☆ ☆ ☆	○ ☆ ☆ ☆ ☆ ☆

19. Please rate your agreement with the following statements.

	Strongly disagree	Disagree	Neutral	Agree	Strongly agree	Not Applicable
I believe free security software is good enough for my daily computing	○	○	○	○	○	○
In general, I trust free security software.	○	○	○	○	○	○

20. When deciding which security software to use, would you consider the country of origin ?
(i.e. country where the vendor is based)

○ Yes

○ No

Section D : Your intention to use security software in the future. D-1

🔲 Hidden unless: Question "Are you currently using security software?" #5 contains any ("Yes")
22. Are you considering changing your current security software?

○ Yes

○ No

D-2

🔲 Hidden unless: (Question "What kind of security software are you using?" #8 contains any ("Free Internet security suite","Free Anti-virus product") AND Question "Are you considering changing your current security software?" #22 contains any ("Yes"))
23. Do you intend to change to paid security software?

○ Yes

○ No

○ Not sure

🔲 Hidden unless: (Question "What kind of security software are you using?" #8 contains any ("Paid Internet security suite","Paid Anti-virus product") AND Question "Are you considering changing your current security software?" #22 contains any ("Yes"))
24. Do you intend to change to free security software?

○ Yes

○ No

○ Not sure

LOGIC Hidden unless: Question "Are you considering changing your current security software?" #22 contains any ("Yes")

25. What are the main reasons for you to change your current security software?

- ☐ Poor protection against malware
- ☐ Too expensive
- ☐ Not easy to use
- ☐ Bad reputation of the company
- ☐ Other [＿＿＿＿＿＿＿＿]

D-3

LOGIC Hidden unless: (Question "What kind of security software are you using?" #8 contains any ("Free Internet security suite","Free Anti-virus product") AND Question "Do you intend to change to paid security software?" #23 contains any ("Yes"))

26. How much are you willing to spend on security software annually? (Per computer)

- ○ Less then €20/$28
- ○ €20/$28 to €39,99/$55.99
- ○ €40/$56 to €49.99/$69.99
- ○ €50/$70 or above

Section E: Mobile security software usage. E-1

27. Which mobile operating system do you mainly use?

- ○ Android
- ○ Windows Phone
- ○ ios/apple
- ○ Blackberry/RIM
- ○ I don't know
- ○ I don't use a smartphone
- ○ Other [＿＿＿＿＿＿＿＿]

28. Are you currently using a mobile security app?

- ○ Yes

- ○ No

Logic Hidden unless: Question "Are you currently using a mobile security app?" #28 contains any ("Yes")

29. What kind of mobile security app are you using?

- ○ Paid security app

- ○ Free security app

Logic Hidden unless: Question "Are you currently using a mobile security app?" #28 contains any ("No")

30. Will you use a mobile security app in the near future?

- ○ Yes

- ○ No

- ○ Not sure

Logic Hidden unless: Question "Will you use a mobile security app in the near future?" #30 contains any ("Yes")

31. What kind of mobile security app do you intend to use?

- ○ Paid security app

- ○ Free security app

Logic Hidden unless: Question "What kind of mobile security app are you using?" #29 contains any ("Paid security app")

32. Do you intend to use a free mobile security app?

- ○ Yes

- ○ No

- ○ Not sure

Logic Hidden unless: Question "What kind of mobile security app are you using?" #29 contains any ("Free security app")

33. Do you intend to use a paid mobile security app?

○ Yes

○ No

○ Not sure

34. Your gender?

○ Male

○ Female

35. Where are you from?

-- Please Select --

36. Your education level?

○ 12th grade or less

○ Graduated high school or equivalent

○ Some college, no degree

○ Bachelor's degree

○ Post-graduate degree

37. Your occupation?

38. What is your monthly income?

Appendix A-2 Summary report of the survey

1. Which operating system do you mainly use?

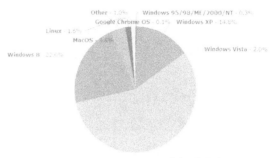

2. Which web browser do you mainly use?

3. How would you describe your level of computer proficiency?

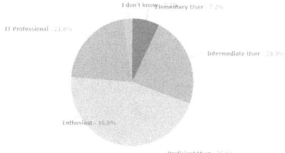

4. How frequently do you use a PC for the following activities?

	At least once a day		At least once a week		At least once a month		Less than once a month		Never		Responses
Entertainment (e.g. media, gaming, internet surfing, social networks)	742	81.7%	119	12.4%	19	2.0%	21	2.2%	16	1.7%	957
Work/business	591	64.9%	156	17.1%	39	4.3%	42	4.6%	83	9.1%	911
Study/research	465	52.1%	280	32.5%	68	7.6%	36	4.0%	33	3.7%	692
Electronic banking (e.g. paying bills, viewing statements, transferring funds)	155	17.2%	378	41.3%	200	22.0%	87	9.6%	90	8.9%	910
Online shopping	81	8.6%	239	25.6%	316	34.4%	215	23.4%	71	7.7%	915
Downloading	402	46.5%	324	35.0%	111	12.0%	60	6.5%	10	1.1%	907

5. Are you currently using security software?

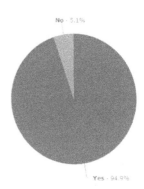

No - 5.1%

Yes - 94.9%

6. Have you ever been the victim of any kind of cyber-crime (e.g. malware infection or hacker attack), or lost personal data (e.g. by hard-disk failure)?

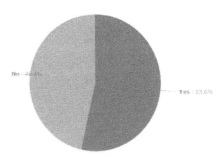

No - 46.4%

Yes - 53.6%

7. How long have you been using security software?

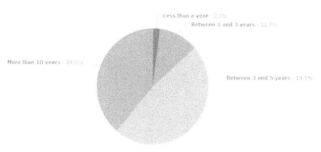

8. What kind of security software are you using?

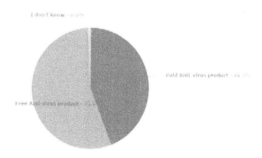

9. How much do you spend per computer on security software annually?

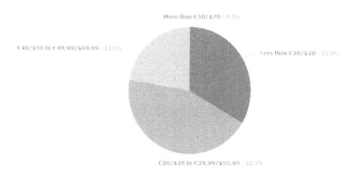

10. Did you know that free antivirus products are available?

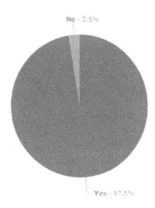

No - 2.5%

Yes - 97.5%

11. Do you intend to start using security software in the near future?

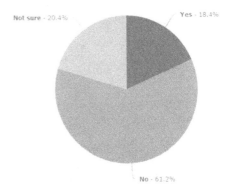

Not sure - 20.4%

Yes - 18.4%

No - 61.2%

12. Why do you prefer to pay for security software rather than use a free program?

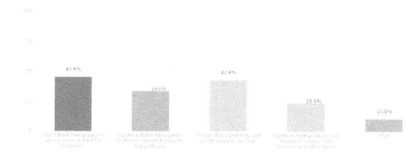

13. When you buying a security software, what kind of packaging do you prefer?

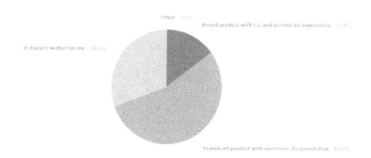

14. Where did you get your security software last time?

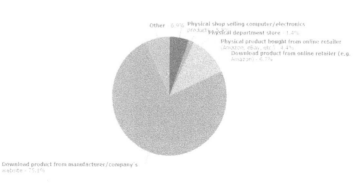

15. If you wanted to buy a new security product, where would you go for advice?

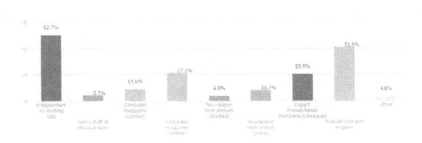

16. How often do you read reviews/test reports before you choose security products?

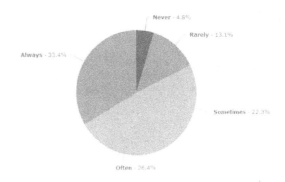

17. How important are the following factors on your choice of security software?

	Not at all important		Not important		Neutral		Important		Very important		Not Applicable		Responsi
Price	46	5.0%	56	6.0%	224	24.2%	277	29.9%	294	31.7%	29	3.1%	926
Protection from malware	9	0.9%	2	0.2%	24	2.5%	142	15.0%	756	79.7%	15	1.6%	948
Ease of installation	67	7.2%	129	13.8%	204	21.8%	280	29.9%	244	26.1%	12	1.3%	936
Ease of use	26	2.8%	59	6.3%	142	15.1%	335	35.5%	370	39.2%	11	1.2%	943
Number of features	33	3.5%	82	8.8%	212	22.6%	297	31.7%	302	32.2%	11	1.2%	937
Suggestion from friends	0	0.0%	0	0.0%	0	0.0%	0	0.0%	0	0.0%	0	0.0%	0
Performance (impact on system speed)	11	1.2%	8	0.8%	53	5.6%	204	21.5%	652	68.8%	19	2.0%	947

18. In your opinion, how well do you think free security software compares with paid-for products?

	Paid security software	Free of charge security software
Protection against malware	★ ★ ★ ★ ☆ ☆ (4.35) Count: 880 StdDev: 0.60 Max: 5	★ ★ ★ ★ ☆ ☆ ☆ (3.65) Count: 903 StdDev: 0.99 Max: 5
Privacy of my data	★ ★ ★ ★ ☆ ☆ (4.13) Count: 870 StdDev: 0.92 Max: 5	★ ★ ★ ☆ ☆ ☆ (3.20) Count: 885 StdDev: 1.16 Max: 5
Ease of use	★ ★ ★ ★ ☆ ☆ (3.92) Count: 867 StdDev: 0.96 Max: 5	★ ★ ★ ★ ☆ ☆ (4.00) Count: 897 StdDev: 0.96 Max: 5
Number of features	★ ★ ★ ★ ☆ ☆ (4.24) Count: 872 StdDev: 0.96 Max: 5	★ ★ ★ ☆ ☆ ☆ (3.33) Count: 897 StdDev: 1.14 Max: 5
Technical support	★ ★ ★ ★ ☆ ☆ (4.29) Count: 864 StdDev: 0.94 Max: 5	★ ★ ★ ☆ ☆ ☆ (2.77) Count: 892 StdDev: 1.26 Max: 5

20. When deciding which security software to use, would you consider the country of origin? (i.e. country where the vendor is based)

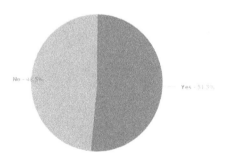

No - 48.5%   Yes - 51.5%

21. Please rate the following countries, on a scale of -3 to +3

	-3 Extremely negative		-2		-1		0		+1		+2		+3 Extremely positive	
Russia	57	12.5%	38	8.4%	45	9.9%	85	18.7%	75	16.5%	79	17.4%	76	16.7%
China	112	23.7%	71	15.0%	54	11.4%	79	16.7%	49	10.4%	40	8.5%	68	14.4%
USA	50	10.9%	26	5.7%	26	5.7%	74	16.2%	76	16.6%	103	22.5%	102	22.3%
Germany	13	2.9%	3	0.7%	6	1.3%	82	18.1%	78	17.3%	131	29.0%	139	30.8%
Romania	51	11.4%	36	8.1%	40	9.0%	169	37.9%	62	13.9%	57	12.8%	31	7.0%
Czech Republic	31	6.9%	24	5.4%	30	6.7%	161	35.9%	79	17.6%	84	18.8%	39	8.7%
Finland	17	3.8%	8	1.8%	10	2.2%	146	32.7%	91	20.4%	95	21.3%	80	17.9%

22. Are you considering changing your current security software?

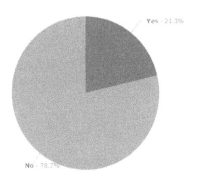

Yes - 21.3%

No - 78.7%

23. Do you intend to change to paid security software?

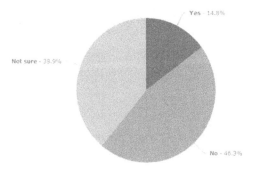

Yes - 14.8%

Not sure - 38.9%

No - 46.3%

24. Do you intend to change to free security software?

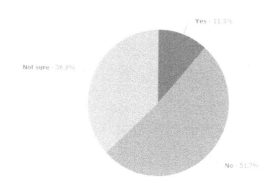

25. What are the main reasons for you to change your current security software?

26. How much are you willing to spend on security software annually? (Per computer)

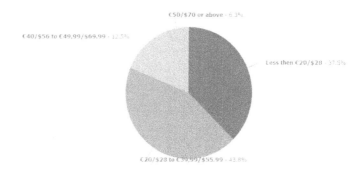

27. Which mobile operating system do you mainly use?

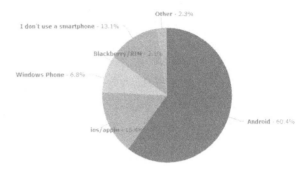

28. Are you currently using a mobile security app?

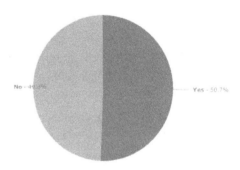

29. What kind of mobile security app are you using?

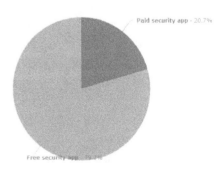

30. Will you use a mobile security app in the near future?

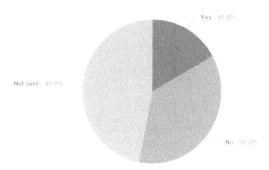

Yes - 16.8%

Not sure - 46.9%

No - 36.2%

31. What kind of mobile security app do you intend to use?

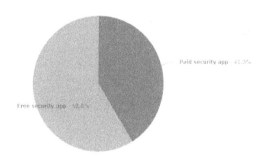

Paid security app - 41.3%

Free security app - 58.8%

32. Do you intend to use a free mobile security app?

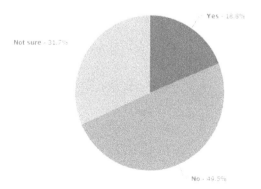

Yes - 18.8%

Not sure - 31.7%

No - 49.5%

33. Do you intend to use a paid mobile security app?

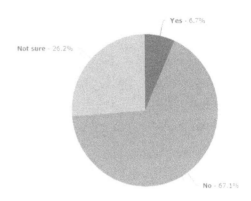

34. Your gender?

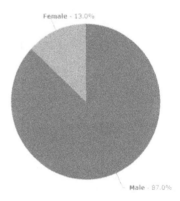

36. Your education level?

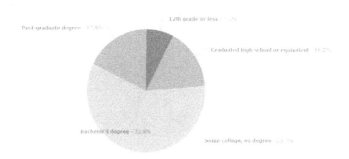

37. Your occupation?

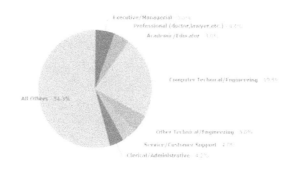

38. What is your monthly income?

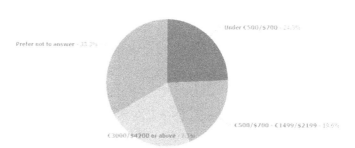

Herstellung und Verlag:
BoD - Books on Demand, Norderstedt
ISBN 978-3-7386-0022-3